THE BEST ARTICLES OF
FR. JOHN T. CATOIR, JCD

To Lito

With fond memories

John Catoir

1/20/22

THE BEST ARTICLES OF
FR. JOHN T. CATOIR, JCD

SMITH & BENJAMIN PUBLISHING

BAHAMAS

Articles	Fr. John T. Catoir, JCD
Compilation of Articles	Marie Sommese Hantak
About the Author	Ashley Rose Olbrich
Editing, Layout & Design	Dionne Benjamin-Smith
Front Cover & Select Photography	Dale Dexter
Back Cover Photograph	Patricia Martin
Vector Art	Vecteezy

Catoir, John T. Fr.
The Best Articles of Fr. John T. Catoir, JCD /
by Fr. John T. Catoir, JCD
ISBN: 978-976-95429-2-1

SMITH & BENJAMIN PUBLISHING

P O BOX CB 12077, NASSAU, THE BAHAMAS · HELLO@SMITH-BENJAMIN.COM

dedication

I dedicate this book to our Blessed Mother Mary, on whose birthday I was privileged to be born.

Also, with great affection, I dedicate this book to my family and friends who have graciously loved and helped me throughout the years. May God richly bless each and every one of you.

Fr. John T. Catoir, JCD
April 2021

acknowledgements

I am happy to acknowledge **the Staff of** *The Beacon,* the Catholic newspaper of the diocese of Paterson, New Jersey, who carried my syndicated columns for well over half a century.

To **Marie Sommese Hantak,** my devoted secretary of many years, who lovingly transcribed and compiled all the articles within this book;

To my beloved niece from The Bahamas, **Dionne Benjamin-Smith** who edited, designed, and published this book of her dear uncle's articles;

To **Ashley Rose Olbrich,** my business manager and Vice President of Saint Jude's Media Ministry Inc., who, with love and great patience, has faithfully managed my business affairs and brought light and laughter to the process.

I humbly and graciously thank you for your loving kindness. May God bless and keep you all in His love always and forever.

Fr. John T. Catoir, JCD
April 2021

December 7, 1994

Dear Friends:

It is with sentiments of profound gratitude that I take this opportunity to publicly thank Father John Catoir for his sixteen years of dedicated service as the Director of the Christophers. Through his creative use of the media, he has touched the lives of thousands of people from all walks of life.

Father Catoir's Ministry of Light has truly brought to life in its fullest sense the meaning of evangelization. The Board of the Christophers acted wisely in appointing him Director Emeritus, and we can look forward to hearing from him in the years ahead.

Father John Catoir has made God's presence felt in so many ways for so many years. I salute him as an example of priestly presence in our midst and ask God to bless his future as he continues to preach the gospel in new and different ways in the Diocese of Paterson, New Jersey.

With best wishes,
        and Faithfully in Christ,

John Cardinal O'Connor
Archbishop of New York

table of contents

About the Author   1

Introduction   5

A God of Surprises   7

A Legacy of Joy   9

A Ministry of Joy   11

Abortion and Divine Mercy   13

Atheism   15

Bear Your Cross with Courage   17

Being an Instrument of God's Love   19

Blessed are the Peacemakers   21

Caring for the Elderly   23

Catholic Thinking   25

Cell-Phone Mania   27

Controlling Your Thoughts   29

Coping with Life   31

Courage and Cowardice   33

Create Your Own Future   35

C. S. Lewis: Why Be Catholic   37

Dementia and Spiritually   39

Divine Mercy   41

Do You Hear the Voice of Love?   43

Don't Worry, Be Happy   45

Dunkirk   47

Easter 2018   49

Evolution Revisited   51

Fear is the Enemy   53

Finding Peace   55

Good Friday   57

God Loves You   59

Happiness: Our Destiny   61

Holy Communion   63

How to Make a Good Retreat   65

Immaturity and Marriage   67

Inner Peace Depends on You   69

Jesus and the Bible   71

Jesus Chose a Married Priesthood   73

Jesus Suffered for Our Sins   75

Joy Prevails Over Sorrow   77

Letting Love in During Lent   79

Major and Minor Addictions   81

Meditations and Loneliness   83

Modern Skepticism and You   85

Mother Theresa and C.S. Lewis   87

My Early Days as a Priest   89

My Father   91

My Favorite Movies   93

My Interview with Mr. Rogers   95

My Vocation   99

Nature vs. Nurture   101

Newman and Your New Year Resolution   103

On Being a Better Pastor   105

Our Father   107

Our Hearts are Restless   109

Pentecost and You   111

Pope Francis   113

Prepare Your Heart for Holiness   115

Private Conscience and the Church   117

Proud to be a Catholic Priest   119

Rejoicing Always is Possible   121

Rich Man, Poor Man   123

Sadness   125

School Shootings   127

Science and Wisdom   129

Securing Our Borders   131

Self-Help is a Choice	133
Sexuality	135
Sir Winston Churchill	137
Some Fear Is Salutary	139
Spiritual Joy Through Daydreaming	141
Stay Calm	143
Tell a Loved One You Care	145
Tell It Like It Is	147
The Afterlife	149
The Battle Against Pedophilia	151
The Birth of Jesus Christ	153
The Bottom Line	155
The Cross and Joy	157
The Fallen Human Race	159
The First Amendment and You	161
The Hidden Hand of God	163
The Joyful Season of Lent	165
The Joy of Forgiveness	167
The Joy of Jesus	169
The Marriage Tribunal	171
The Optimism of Pope John XXIII	173
The Priesthood and the Laity	175
There's Nobody Like You	177
The Theology of Christmas	179
The Will Says Yes or No	181
Transformation in Christ	183
Understanding God's Mercy	185
What Does Jesus Ask of You	187
What God Has Brought Together	189
When a Workaholic Retires	191
You and Your Bible	193
Your Higher Calling	195
Your New Year's Resolutions	197
Your Tax Dollar	199

about the author

F ather John Thomas Catoir was born on September 8th, 1931 in Manhattan, New York to John T. Catoir, Sr. (Jack) and Catherine M. Caslin (Kitty). September 8th is the birthday of the Blessed Mother for whom Fr. John has always had a special devotion. He, along with his younger sister Catherine, grew up in his parents' loving care in Jackson Heights, Queens, New York. He attended St. Joan of Arc Grammar School and later studied with the Jesuits graduating from Brooklyn Prep and Fordham University School of Business with a Bachelor of Science degree in Economics. He rose to be president of his senior classes in both schools.

In 1953, John graduated from Fordham University and with the Korean War winding down, he was drafted into the U.S. Army and became a member of the Military Police at Fort Sam Houston in San Antonio, Texas. After serving one year as an MP, the Catholic Chaplain – Maj. George Phillips – asked him to be his assistant. It was during that final year of working for the Chaplain that John decided to enter the seminary to become a priest. In 1960, he was ordained.

Soon after Fr. John's ordination, Bishop McNulty of Paterson, New Jersey sent him to Catholic University to earn a doctorate degree in canon law. When he returned with his JCD degree, he was put in charge of the diocesan Marriage Tribunal where he served in the capacity of Judicial Vicar for many years. He also served as pastor of Our Lady of Victories, an inner parish in Paterson.

When the priests of the Paterson diocese elected Fr. John to be their first full-time clergy personnel director, a job in which he assisted the Bishop in the assignment and placement of priests, he had to leave his work in the Tribunal. Three years later, he was elected President of NACPA, the National Association of Church Personnel Administrators, where he helped formulate experimental ministries on the national level.

Fr. John became Director of The Christophers in 1978 when the organization's board invited him to be their Chairman & CEO after their founder, Maryknoll Father James Keller, had passed away just the year before in 1977. Fr. John accepted the position and moved into his office in Manhattan to begin a new career in the world of radio and TV.

For the next 17 years, Fr. John hosted his own nationally syndicated TV interview show called *Christopher Closeup*. During that period he wrote his syndicated column and was elected President of the Catholic Press Associations of both the United States and Canada which gave him their highest award – The St. Francis de Sales Award.

For Fr. John, writing was a vocation within a vocation. Over the past 60+ years, he has written 20 books and countless articles that have been syndicated by The Catholic Press Association. Most of his books focused on the theme of Joy and were written while he was Director of The Christophers, including the popular *Three Minutes a Day* series.

Social media soon became fascinating to Fr. John and he jumped in with both feet. He created a blog entitled messengerofjoy.com as well as an eponymous website: www.johncatoir.com — both offering daily meditations on Joy to millions of viewers all over America and beyond. Many of these can be viewed on his own YouTube channel.

In 1995, Fr. John founded St. Jude Media Ministry, Inc. to continue this social media outreach under his own control. Gradually, he expanded his participation by joining Facebook and Twitter on which he posts thousands of spiritually-oriented Tweets worldwide, all of which are aimed at lifting the spirits of readers and proclaiming the truth that Jesus came to bring joy.

Fr. John's final years of active ministry were spent doing work amongst the hungry, poverty-stricken, and those suffering from addiction. In 1997, the Board of Directors of Eva's Village in Paterson, New Jersey—one of the largest poverty programs in the U.S. with men's and women's shelters and a soup kitchen feeding 1,000 meals a day—invited him to be their new executive director.

Still active in his role as Director of St. Jude Media, Fr. John was delighted to accept this invitation and joyfully served Eva's Village for three years until, suddenly, cancer entered into his life.

Fr. John had to retire from Eva's Village in the year 2000 at the age of 70, due to prostate cancer surgery. However, he continued to write his nationally-syndicated column for the Catholic Press for many more years.

In 2017, The Catholic Press Association established *The John Catoir Award* in his honor for *Best Use of Social Media in Evangelization.* The award was aimed at making Jesus better known and loved.

Fr. John lived in community with his brother priests in retirement for 12 years until he needed an assisted-living facility which brought him to the warmer climate of North Carolina.

In his 90s, Fr. John continues to express his heartfelt gratitude to everyone who has helped him throughout his entire life. He always closes his letters with these words: "May the Lord be your strength and your joy."

Ashley Rose Olbrich
Vice President
St. Jude Media Ministry, Inc.

introduction

MY ADMIRATION FOR POPE FRANCIS
By Fr. John T. Catoir, JCD | February 27, 2018

Pope Francis has my admiration because I hear the voice of love speaking through him. He always stresses God's mercy and has the courage to take on canonical legalists who find the mystery of Divine Mercy too difficult to fit into their mentality.

"For God did not send His Son to the world to condemn it, but to save it." (John 3:17). Mercy seems like laxity to the conservative prelates who became alarmed when Pope Francis urged Catholics to rely more on their conscience in resolving personal moral issues.

Having been the Judicial Vicar of my Diocese for many years, I experienced how imperfect the Marital Tribunal system was. When I became its Chief Judge, I came across many cases where annulments were denied unjustly because of poorly run courts, and because of an overly rigid application of the rules of evidence. Very few annulments were granted in the 1960s and 1970s.

After receiving my doctorate in canon law and when I came home to run the Diocesan Tribunal, I often had to tell the aggrieved parties that following their inner sense of the truth as they stand before God was often more reliable than being sent away with a questionable verdict. When Pope Francis was elected, it wasn't long before he began urging Catholics to rely more on their conscience, and that was music to my ears. Reliance on conscience is an established principle of Moral Theology.

Father Federico Lombardi, the Vatican spokesperson at the time, reported that Pope Francis was saying that in grave situations, a well-formed conscience can be relied upon. The gravity of the situation was to be determined by the parties themselves.

Pope Francis, born in Argentina on Dec. 17, 1936, was elected Pope on March 13, 2013. He was the first Latin American Pope, the first Jesuit Pope and the first non-European Pope in 1,000 years.

On July 29, 2013, he said, "If someone is gay, and sincerely searches for the Lord, and has good will – who am I to judge?" He immediately got into trouble for that quote, but the Catholic parents of gay children felt genuine solace. While he did not endorse same sex marriage, he did say there could be some sort of civil union to protect their civil rights.

Conservative Catholics become fearful that any relaxation of the laws pertaining to marriage and divorce or contraception would threaten the Church's broader stance on medical ethics and sexual issues. This is an understandable concern, but not an insurmountable one. Freedom of conscience is a human right.

Pope Paul VI affirmed the immoral nature of artificial contraception in his Encyclical, *Humanae Vitae*. Pope Francis has remained firm in his opposition to those who refuse to have children because it interferes with their lifestyle, but he respects the consciences of those who are struggling to raise children in today's world.

Pope Francis agrees with the various National Hierarchies that have instructed their laity that the use of private conscience in these matters is permissible. He also highlighted Paul VI's instruction to priests, urging them to show compassion in the confessional in these matters.

What I admire about Pope Francis is his willingness to bring all this into public debate. Affirming freedom of conscience is an act of intellectual honesty and a way of being both merciful and understanding. These are God-like qualities.

God bless Pope Francis.

A GOD OF SURPRISES

By Fr. John T. Catoir, JCD | September 10, 2017

A reader of my columns wrote me this interesting note: "We certainly have a God of surprises! I have a story to tell you. Every week I go to my local library and often find a treasure. Today I found an old Catholic Bible which I couldn't resist. I took it home and guess what fell out of it? An old column of yours!"

She continued, "As if this surprise wasn't enough, when I read the article, I realized it was meant just for me! Even though it was written many years ago, it touched my life right now. Wow!"

She sent the article to me, but didn't indicate the problem she was dealing with. Nevertheless, I saw the substance of it was generic enough to help others. It was entitled: "Depend on God". It was about assigning a specific role to God in the solution of any problem. There's a difference between praying for God's help and assigning Him a specific role in the solution of the problem.

Coping with any troubling problem should always begin with a prayer and a question: "Am I really going to rely on God's strength? How much will I depend on God and how much will I depend on myself? Too much self-reliance can get you into trouble. Those who think they can go it alone are dead in the water.

It's quite normal to roll up your sleeves to do battle; however, if you try to do too much on your own, you may regret it. Some problems are merely irksome, but others are beyond your direct control. For instance, an alcoholic spouse is a problem you must treat with care and wisdom.

There's no way you can make another person change. With the help of God, they must change themselves. Alcoholics and all others who are chemically dependent, know that they cannot rely on their own will-power. Only when they call upon God to supply supernatural strength can the recovery process begin in a meaningful way.

First, they must volunteer to practice the Third Step. Here's my paraphrase of it: 'Because I am powerless over my addiction, I am turning my life and my will over to the God of my understanding. God is all-powerful. With that in mind, I hereby turn over to Him all responsibility for my sobriety. I know that He will do for me what I am not yet able to do for myself.

Does that sound too bold? It isn't! Millions of sober men and women, who call themselves 'recovering' alcoholics or addicts, can attest to the fact that God took away the cravings that obsessed them. Somehow, they shed the pain of constant failure and began to feel free again.

If you feel powerless over a problem, turn it over to the One who has all the power. "Come to me all you who are weary and burdened, and I will give you rest." (Matthew 11:29)

Let go of it and hope for the best.

A LEGACY OF JOY

By Fr. John T. Catoir, JCD | May 11, 2017

A legacy is defined as something handed down by a predecessor. When I think about the concept of spiritual joy, I see it as a legacy handed down to us by the Lord Himself. Jesus wants you to receive His joy and pass it along to others. Pope St. John Paul II, said, "Go therefore and become messengers of joy."

I wrote a book entitled *Enjoy The Lord* which was reprinted in seven languages. This led to my trilogy on Joy: *Enjoy The Lord, God Delights in You,* and *Enjoy Your Precious Life* — all from Alba House, New York. The demand for these books taught me that there is a deep hunger out there for more information on the topic of spiritual joy. *(Editor's Note: not all of these books are still available).*

Let's face it, the Catholic Church and many other Christian churches of the past were filled with fear and foreboding. Damnation was a constant theme. Mortal sins were considered as easy to commit as eating meat on Friday or missing Mass on Sunday. Even when legitimate excuses existed, people felt guilty. I remember hearing the confession of a woman who missed Sunday Mass twice in a row. I asked her why? She replied, "I was in the hospital having a baby and there were complications." I told her there was no sin in that. She said, "I just wanted to be safe."

Fear of Divine punishment was a constant theme and the punishment for mortal sin was eternal damnation. When you put that kind of thinking up against the words of Jesus who said, "I have told you all these things that your joy may be full..." (John 15:11), you can better understand the issue. Jesus wasn't merely speaking of our heavenly reward, He was talking about a grace-filled life of joy – here and now. Spiritual Joy is a gift of the Holy Spirit. We can only advance in that gift by putting on the will to trust God's love, and deep and abiding mercy for all His children. "Do not be afraid" was repeated by Jesus many times. St. Paul said, "Rejoice always, and in all circumstances, give thanks to the Lord, for this is the will of God for you in Christ Jesus." (I Thessalonians 5:16-18) The Scriptures tell us that God wants us to find our strength and joy in Him. He told us to, "Fear not." His infinite love and mercy are always with us.

Recently, I wrote a column entitled, *The Optimism of Pope John XXIII* extolling his positive attitude. He relied on the Holy Spirit and was able to stand up to the opposition he received from many Cardinals. When Vatican Council II opened the floodgates of reform, the Church began moving from fear to joy. Even though the Church has always preached mercy and forgiveness, the mentality of fear has diminished considerably due to the influence of all our recent Popes from John to Francis.

Some complain that this spirit of love has led to laxity. A decline in Mass attendance has occurred. But I ask you, which is better: to have attendance at Mass higher because those attending are in fear of God's eternal punishment? Or, having smaller crowds attending Mass because they trust God, and want to receive His loving sustenance?

A MINISTRY OF JOY

By Fr. John T. Catoir, JCD | August 12, 2018

Jesus inspired me with His words, "I have told you all these things that My joy may be in you and your joy may be complete." I took those words and combined them with this quote from a 15th century mystic, Blessed Julian of Norwich, "The greatest honor you can give to Almighty God is to live joyfully because of the knowledge of His love."

In 1995, after I stepped down as Director of The Christophers, I started a new ministry of Joy, and named it after St. Jude. I remembered conducting a St. Jude Novena for many years when I was the pastor at Our Lady of Victories Parish in Paterson, New Jersey. We had a steady flow of devotees attending the Novena which we conducted five times a day on every Thursday. During that period, I witnessed so many miracles of healing, that I gained great confidence in the power of St. Jude's intercession. So, I decided to make him the patron saint of my new ministry. Then we created a new website: messengerofjoy.com to make available a blog which presents daily meditations on joy. Soon after, I added a radio ministry and began recording uplifting radio spots using the words of Jesus and the saints to spread the Gospel message of Joy. With the help of some generous friends we bought air-time and began broadcasting them nationally.

We did this for 17 years until a new electronic miracle came along called Social Media, which gave us access to a worldwide audience at no cost. We were already touching millions of lives worldwide, but I saw that we could reach millions more.

When the time was right, in 2013, I hired Patricia Martin, a social media expert from Dallas, Texas. Together we added a Facebook and

Twitter account and opened a new webpage: www.johncatoir.com and loaded it with my videos from The Christopher days, along with my articles and tweets. In our most recent prayer marathon entitled *Joy to the World,* we had 2.5 million participants.

The combined use of all our Social Media outlets has been spreading Christ's message of joy all over the world for many years. The Catholic Press Association recently created a new annual award: The Father John Catoir Social Media and Evangelization Award. I thank God and the Association and St. Jude, the Patron saint of hopeless cases.

Let's all pray for the grace to live joyfully in the present moment, not in stewing over the past, or worrying about the future but staying in the present moment. Here is a favorite prayer of mine to help you along the way:

> "Dear Holy Spirit, Soul of my soul, protect me, console me and tell me what to do as I strive to live in the present moment. Let me know Your will and give me the strength to follow it. St. Teresa of Avila used to repeat the following mantra to herself over and over: 'Let nothing disturb you; let nothing cause you fear. God is always at your side protecting you. God is unchanging love.'"

ABORTION AND DIVINE MERCY

By Fr. John T. Catoir, JCD | May 1, 2018

In this column, I want to reach out to all women, especially those who have had an abortion. Without diminishing the seriousness of the sin, I want to tell them about the Good News of the Gospel.

I'll begin with this universal truth: "Never put a limit on God's Mercy." You've heard it said that God is Love. Well it's true. God's Love is infinite, unconditional, and unchanging. Do not live in some dark corner apart from His loving kindness.

There are no unforgivable sins. The only sin called unforgivable in the Gospels is the sin of refusing God's forgiveness. A person who refuses to accept God's forgiveness cannot receive it. The main point, however, is that God wipes away all the sins of everyone who repents and asks Him for forgiveness. As far as worrying about the baby's well-being, you must leave it up to God to shower him or her with love.

When I hear confessions, I conclude with these words, "You've made a good confession; now put your mind at ease and try as best you can to trust God's love completely. For now, renew your good intentions and go in peace."

At a recent White House Press Corps dinner, the entertainer made jokes about yanking her baby out of her womb. She even used the word "baby". Watching an audience laughing at this kind of humor was horrifying. Mother Theresa and millions of saints in heaven must have been outraged. So were millions of Americans of all faiths. There is nothing funny about abortion.

It's difficult to write about Divine Mercy on this topic. It seems like you're downplaying the magnitude of the evil. I tried it once many years ago, and to my utter shock the article was used in abortion clinics to encourage women to proceed with their abortion. That's like trying to get absolution before you kill someone.

I've been wary ever since. Even so, I've risked it again today because I fully realize that many women were almost paralyzed with fear when they aborted their child; a deed they detested in their heart of hearts. They did not give full consent of their will.

Permit me to conclude with a mini lesson in moral culpability. Men who force women into having an abortion are guilty of murder. In such circumstances, the women are often more sinned against than anything else. A mortal sin requires serious matter, sufficient reflection, and full consent of the will. The murder of a human being is a serious matter. But many women are pressured into it without sufficient reflection and full consent of the will. Some cowardly man or family member pushed them into it, and without the necessary support system they succumbed to misery.

Permit me to conclude, I think that's why Pope Francis tempered the zeal of those who make abortion the central issue of Christian revelation. Their condemnations are too sweeping.

Brava to those heroic women who found the moral strength to save their baby in such extreme circumstances. To all men and women, I send the assurance of Divine Love.

> "May the passion and death of Our Lord Jesus Christ, the merits of the Blessed Virgin Mary and all the saints, and whatsoever good you do, or suffering you endure, may it lead to the remission of your sins, the increase of grace, and the gift of everlasting life with God in heaven."

ATHEISM
By Fr. John T. Catoir, JCD | January 11, 2018

Recently, I came across an amusing cartoon depicting two snowmen; one was rebuking the other. The caption read, "Don't be absurd! Of course, no one made us! We evolved from random snowflakes."

Poking fun at Darwin's theory of evolution is considered irreverent in some circles, but I take delight in it. His theory gave so much comfort to atheists in their effort to deny God's existence. I gladly admit that the theory of evolution is a scientific fact, but this in no way proves that God does not exist.

Albert Einstein and I do not understand how a serious person can deny the necessity of the existence of a supreme intelligence behind the cosmos. But that's just us. We believe there are many ways of knowing: rational deduction is one and intuition is another. Albert thrived on intuition.

Atheists are quick to dismiss these tried and true methods, saying that the burden of proof is on the believer to prove scientifically that God exists. No problem! I am pleased to tell you that there is new scientific evidence that is helping us to understand some very important theological truths. Permit me to share a quote from a mathematical physicist named Dr. Frank Tipler of Tulane University. His book is entitled, *The Physics of Immortality*.

Doctor Tipler wrote, "When I began my career as a cosmologist some twenty years ago, I was a convinced atheist. I never in my wildest dreams imagined that one day I would be writing a book purporting to show that the central claims of Judeo-Christian theology are, in fact, true. And that these claims are straightforward deductions of the laws of physics as we now understand them. I have been forced into these conclusions by the inexorable logic of my own special branch of physics."

Wow! The usual claim of science that the existence of God cannot be scientifically proven has now been discredited by many professional physicists. Check out Google, and you'll find 40 quotes that were made by former atheists who are now believers. They talk about the folly of denying God's existence. Those who deny this essential truth in the name of science are performing an act of deliberate inadvertence.

This new understanding has affected my attitude toward atheists in general. I now find their hubris a bit sad. How can a serious person conclude that a random scattering of atoms accidently fell together to form our complex universe? One cannot even imagine the possibility of it.

Common sense is at play here. Walt Whitman, in his poem *Leaves of Grass,* wrote, "A single mouse is miracle enough to convert a thousand infidels." No one should defy right reason. Especially since we now see that the higher levels of physics are compelling many to admit that God must exist. Of course, you knew that, but those who denied this fundamental truth for years can no longer claim to be intellectually superior; quite the opposite.

I intend no personal disrespect toward atheists in general. My effort is to discredit the atheistic movement. There are many atheists who are good human beings and who have shown real charity to those in need; perhaps more than you might suspect. I just want to help them find their way home, and to discover the joys of living a life of faith.

May the Lord be your strength and your joy.

BEAR YOUR CROSS WITH COURAGE

By Fr. John T. Catoir, JCD | March 10, 2019

Faith can move mountains. Such a feat is only possible with the help of faith. The same is true about living joyfully because of the knowledge of God's love. It's a lot easier than most people think. All you need to do is put on the will to bear discomfort. Through God's grace you can do all things. Faith gives us all a huge advantage over those who never ask God for help. They live as though they have no faith at all.

Here are a few ideas that will help you to keep from being discouraged, especially in times of suffering. Even Jesus had to pray for help in accepting His cross. "If it be possible Father, take this cross from me, but not my will but thine be done." God's grace brings a quiet uncomplaining spirit during times of pain. Jesus may not take your suffering away all at once; but He will fill your pain with His presence. Unite your suffering to His, and you automatically live a life of Faith.

Suffering is the coin that purchased our redemption. It's always working for you, never against you. You may not be able to understand this concept fully, but God is always there with you, giving your suffering greater meaning as it becomes part of the redemptive process. When your pain and suffering become unbearable, you have two choices: suicide or holiness. Suicide is no solution; you'll set a terrible example for everyone and you'll regret it for all eternity.

Therefore, decide to be a saint.

God invites you to bear pain for a redemptive purpose. Accept His permissive will in this matter and it will not only lift your spirit, but it will enable you to inspire others by your courage. For every pain we must bear, there's a reason, and God knows the reason. So, take your courage from the Lord and learn to suffer in silence. By that I mean, be kind to your caregivers. Suffering in silence is an act of charity toward your caregivers. Patients should always strive to be patient. Don't be a constant complainer.

Many saints prayed for the gift of martyrdom, knowing that it might entail great suffering. I'd advise you to keep it simple. Understand that true prayer is found in the will to give yourself to God. Let's all pray for the grace to live joyfully, not worrying about the past or the future. Here's a favorite payer of mine:

"Dear Holy Spirit, Soul of my soul, protect me as I strive to live in the present moment. Let me know your will and give me the strength to follow it."

This too is a favorite prayer taken from the final prayer at the Mass on Sunday, March 10, 2019:

"May bountiful blessings, O Lord we pray, come down on your people, that hope may grow in tribulation, and that virtue be strengthened in temptation, and that eternal redemption be assured forever, through Christ Our Lord, Amen."

BEING AN INSTRUMENT OF GOD'S LOVE

By Fr. John T. Catoir, JCD | August 22, 2006

God is love. Benjamin Franklin once said, "Wine is proof that God loves us and wants us to be happy." I like that kind of simplicity. A divine mystery is not easily explained.

But for those who may want a more theological answer, here is my humble effort. Keep in mind that theology is a science, which tries to explain the unexplainable.

There are three Persons in God: Father, Son, and Holy Spirit. The Spirit is described as "the Love" passing between the Father and the Son. In this context, Love is not only a Divine Person, but also an action.

Jesus promised to leave us the Holy Spirit after he ascended into heaven. And thus, the Spirit is continually active among us, especially in the Sacraments of the Church.

The Spirit of Jesus acts in every sacrament. Always remember that wherever one Person of the Trinity is present, all three are present. In this way, God infuses His life into us, giving us the hope and courage, we need to become instruments of His love.

The Holy Spirit has often been compared to a great wind that carries us along. We do not tell the wind where to blow. All we can do is set our sails to catch the wind and allow ourselves to be led in the direction chosen for us. This direction, however, might be one we would not have chosen for ourselves. Our foreign missionaries often end up in distant lands because of the Holy Spirit. I heard one priest say, "How did a guy like me end up in Peru?"

Mother Teresa said, "Christ often comes to us in distressing disguises." Suppose the Spirit wanted to show his love for a mentally sick person by using you as His instrument. This person might be put in your life as a test; to see how you might react. You can walk away, or you can accept the challenge of the cross. Love leads to service, and service usually leads to the cross.

You will need a strategy if you want to be effective. To begin with, do not overestimate your capacity to bring about any kind of healing. God can do all things, but you can't. Healing takes time. Try not to blame the disturbed person for not trying hard enough to get well. This will only be taken as an attack, and serve no useful purpose. For all you know the person's mental state might be due to a brain tumor.

Keep this formula in mind: "If you abuse me, you lose me." If the person abuses you or tends to reject you, reevaluate your mission. Never allow anyone to abuse you. Sick people are not excused from the obligation to be charitable. Bad behavior should not be rewarded. You may have to break away from the situation. If so, do it in slow stages, without feeling guilty about it. If you threaten to withdraw, very often the person adjusts.

You have to love yourself, and that means you have to demand respect from others. At this point, turn the whole problem over to the Holy Spirit.

In the end, you will be judged on your effort to be an instrument of God's love, not on your success or failure. This is true in failed marriages as well.

Jesus loved well, but He was completely rejected, abused, and crucified.

The servant is not greater than the Master.

BLESSED ARE THE PEACEMAKERS

By Fr. John T. Catoir, JCD | February 5, 2019

Peacemakers include all those honorable law enforcement officers, male and female, who dedicate their lives, day-in and day-out, to keeping the peace. Having once served as a Military Policeman in the U.S. Army, I experienced the ordeal of performing the many duties of law enforcement. Keeping the peace often involves an officer in violent conflicts with drunks, troublemakers, and sometimes more serious criminals.

When Jesus said, "Blessed are the merciful," he wasn't saying that we should abandon the strict enforcement of the law by not holding anyone responsible for disturbing the peace. Police officers must oppose unruly and villainous behavior with courage.

Those who put their lives on the line to prevent criminals from

sinning against law-abiding citizens are heroes, not warmongers. Protecting the rights of the weak is a noble profession. They are the brave men and women who serve their neighbors and their country by risking life and limb every day. Jesus said, "There is no greater love than to lay down one's life for another." And their service runs that risk every day.

Jesus also said, "Blessed are those who hunger and thirst for justice." He was praising those who struggle to promote justice and He promised them that one-day their hunger for justice would be satisfied. Perfect justice may not easily be attained in this world, but God blesses those who strive. They try to build a just society based on their fidelity to the goal of attaining the common good.

Mercy is the name of love when it confronts misery, but vigilance is the name for love when it confronts danger. Protecting others often involves risking one's own personal well-being. Mercy is never an invitation to thugs to misbehave. Threatening the peace of our fellow citizens is a criminal act. Justice requires a duty-bound resistance to evil. An act of obedience to law enforcement is always right and just. It cracks down on mobsters who engage in anti-social criminal behavior, and demands the protection of the innocent. We all must do our part in upholding the common good.

In the book of Micah 6:8, we read this fundamental moral precept: "Act justly, love tenderly, and walk humbly with your God." Jesus defined all of revelation as having a common purpose. "I have told you all this. so that My joy may be in you and your joy may be complete." (John 15:11)

Going forward, I think our law enforcement forces deserve real fairness. Yes, there have been abuses and they must be swiftly corrected. For the most part that has been done. But an atmosphere of fairness requires more. It calls for cooperation and respect. An enormous good has been accomplished in our law enforcement efforts. With the right attitude, we can all benefit from a more peaceful and joyful society. People of all faiths and nationalities need to be their own best friend and not their own worst enemy. With God's help, we can all try to quiet our souls and work together to help make this a better world.

We need to remember to pray. I like this one; "Hail Mary, full of grace, pray for us sinners, now and at the hour of our death, Amen."

May the Lord be your strength and your joy.

CARING FOR THE ELDERLY

By Fr. John T. Catoir, JCD | June 4, 2017

Father's Day has come and gone. Was it a pleasant experience? Have you ever tried to take a grandparent out to a nice restaurant, only to meet strong resistance? "I don't want to go out!" You may find yourself reacting inwardly: 'How ungrateful can you be!'

It's human for you to react that way. Brush off their abruptness as the new normal, and try to understand their way of thinking. Here's the first rule: avoid dropping in without calling first. Always ask what he or she wants before you present your idea for a fun day. Never press your plan. Accept their wishes peacefully.

Accepting the elderly as they are is a good start. Stay calm. If you're dealing with a severe case of second-childhood, be firm. You are now the parent, so insist on their good behavior. Everyone has the same obligation to be as charitable as possible. They must learn patience, and you must remain in charge.

This is all easier said than done, but it's basically common sense. I learned a lot about caring for the elderly when I was 25. I got a job in a New York City hospital, Elmhurst General, and worked as a nurse's aide. They didn't know that I was a seminarian. I was on a summer break doing this as part of my preparation for the priesthood.

The office assigned me to the Male Geriatric Unit, and there I experienced elderly patients who were nice most of the time, but also demanding and mischievous. They all hated losing control and could become obnoxious at times, creating problems for the staff.

Frustration is a part of the human condition. We all try to stay calm, but to err is human. I'm writing this column with the hope that I can be of some help in explaining why the elderly can become irascible for what you might think is a very petty reason.

People who once had authority in business, the military, education, home-making, who gradually begin losing their hearing, their memory, and their power to come and go as they please, often become contrary and irksome. The key to dealing with them is heroic patience. Put on the will to eat humble pie. They all want to be independent, but they know they can't be.

I'm 86 years young at this writing and I have observed my own changing moods and attitudes over the years. At this age, I can become needlessly impatient over insignificant things that never bothered me. I call this stage of life: the disintegration process. Others refer to it as "aging." It can be both pleasant and difficult at the same time.

Pleasant because it's God's will, and it's a normal part of life. And difficult because it's not your will, and it doesn't feel normal.

To all you super-senior citizens whom I love dearly, I say: Pray for the grace to be grateful in all circumstances. No one's perfect so you'll find there will be times when you'll want to scream with indignation. Count to ten, and pray for the strength to be nice. Remember, with God, all things are possible

May the Lord be your strength and your joy.

CATHOLIC THINKING

By Fr. John T. Catoir, JCD | May 12, 2017

In 1965, the Second Vatican Council explained Catholic thinking in this way: "Since Sacred Scripture must be read and interpreted by the same Holy Spirit by whom it was written, one must take into account, in order to draw out the correct sense of the sacred texts, the Tradition of the whole Church." Tradition is important because it protects historical accuracy.

We can count on the correct interpretation of the Lord's words; for instance, from the Last Supper to this very day, Catholics have known that Jesus Christ is truly present in the Eucharist. "This is my Body." (Matthew 26:26)

In the 16th century, the Reformers denied this truth saying that it was only a matter of subjective belief. Not so! The People of God have always believed that Jesus is truly present in the Eucharist. This belief has been kept intact precisely by the guidance of the Holy Spirit through the teaching authority of the Church.

Jesus said this to St. Peter, our first Pope, "He who hears you, hears me." (Luke 10:16) This raises the question, who is Jesus Christ? Non-believers maintain that Jesus was an itinerant rabbi, a political rebel, but nothing more. The Church, however, has always taught that Jesus Christ is true God and true man. We genuflect before the tabernacle. In the Gospel of John 3:16, we read, "God sent His only begotten Son that the world may be saved through Him." Jesus Christ is Our Supreme Lord and Savior. He is God incarnate.

Secularists reject this truth, and refuse to be bound by any religious scruples. They brush aside the faith as fantasy. Their attacks, and those of the Atheist community, are based on their total denial of God. The Church rightly considers their views to be heretical. We can only pray for them, and try to follow the example of Jesus, who prayed for His enemies and forgave His persecutors, "Forgive them Father, for they know not what they do." (Luke 23:34)

We strive to love one another. We care for the least among us as we bring God's message of love to everyone we meet. St. Augustine said, "We are an Easter people, and Alleluia is our song." Jesus taught us that our lives on earth are a prelude to the joys of heaven. Death, therefore, is not the tragedy it appears to be. One could rightly say that death is an illusion. We pass from this world to the next, believing in the promises of Christ.

We are Children of the Light. The Church's teaching authority helps us to transcends the darkness of this world. By God's grace we have received an accurate understanding of supernatural revelation. The call to live joyfully is the final piece of the puzzle. Jesus pronounced His mission in this way, "I have come that my joy may be in you, and that your joy may be complete." (John 15:11)

Pope St. John Paul II has emphasized joy as he summarized the teachings of Jesus: "Joy is the keynote message of Christianity and the recurring motif of the Gospel. Go, therefore, and become messengers of joy."

May the Lord be your strength and your joy.

CELL PHONE MANIA

By Fr. John T. Catoir, JCD | May 3, 2016

Cell phone mania has become a serious epidemic. It even threatens our spiritual well-being. Please give me a minute to explain.

A neighbor gave her 14-year-old daughter a birthday party, and noticed how quiet everyone was. She went into the room, and found them all on their cell phone. She was shocked and immediately reacted. "Put down those phone right now; this is supposed to be a party! Have some fun!," she said. Later, after her daughter's initial embarrassment, they all became normally boisterous and had a happy time.

Fr. John taking a short break to Tweet.
(Photo: Dale Dexter)

The practice of zoning out during family meals in order to use a cell phone is discourteous and unacceptable. Dinner is family time. It should be a loving exchange of ideas and a sharing of feelings. Today the family meal is treated by some as a pit stop. Youngsters have more important things on their minds than family unity. There should be a rule in every home: No cell phone for one hour during the family meal. Family comes first.

Jesus said, "Love one another." St. Peter added, "Be of one mind, love one another as brothers; be courteous." Courtesy is defined as the politeness of one's attitude and behavior toward others. This implies good manners, civility, and respect.

One of the more serious repercussions is automobile accidents caused by the practice of texting while driving. Texting while driving is a sin. We have always been taught not to put ourselves in the occasion of sin. To do so makes us vulnerable to possible disaster. Unnecessary risks are a sinful choice.

You may question my use of the word sin in this connection, but all sin involves actions that are displeasing to God. He loves you, and sin is doing something that hurts the one He loves. We commit many sins of deliberate inadvertence. Parents need to assert their authority more in this area, and insist upon courtesy in all things. No cell phones during the dinner hour.

Have you ever noticed how doctors seem to focus more on record-keeping than on the patient. They open the laptop, type in some statistics, and while still looking at the screen, ask a few questions without looking up. Eventually they do look at you and say a few words, but before you know it, the visit is over. Are doctors losing the art of courtesy?

Mr. Abraham Nussbaum, author of *The Finest Traditions of My Calling*, wrote in the Wall Street Journal, May 5, 2016, "Many doctors are burning out, and advising against a medical career." He blamed it on their scientific approach to medicine, and recommended that doctors revive their commitment to the Hippocratic Oath, which ends, "May I always act so as to preserve the finest traditions of my calling, and may I experience the joy of healing those who seek my help." This quote moved me deeply.

Since Jesus said, "I've come that your joy may be full," I wonder how He must feel about so many of his children becoming addicted to their cell phones. It seems clear to me that our electronic toys and tools are slowly diminishing our sensitivity to the feelings of others. Charity begins at home.

CONTROLLING YOUR THOUGHTS

By Fr. John T. Catoir, JCD | June 11, 2019

Do you suffer from disturbing or obsessive thoughts? If so, relief is available. It will be an uphill battle, but with perseverance and the help of God, it's a battle that's worthwhile because it can be won.

The worst attacks come during the night when you're trying to go to sleep. Some cases are worse than others. The trick is to divert the troubling thoughts by replacing them with something else. Even if the thought persists, perseverance will one day win the war.

Here is how to begin. When you're trying to go to sleep and a troubling thought invades your mind, deflect your attention from it by concentrating on your own breathing. Repeat one word: 'inhale'. Don't force feelings of any kind – and stay relaxed.

As long as your will is occupied on another task, the obsessive thoughts will be held at bay. Choose a sweet thought or beautiful picture to replace it. A sleeping pill will be helpful until the annoyance subsides.

There are also other more important remedies you may need in order to deal with the root cause of a problem. If you suffer from envy, which is sadness or anger over the good fortune of another, you will need to repent, otherwise the attacks will increase. It's a matter of breaking a bad habit.

Any vice, like anger, that has become a habit will make your life a needless ordeal. Put on the will to break the habit. It can and must be done. Your weakness is making your life a needless ordeal. The same is true if you are a vindictive person, when anger begins to seek revenge.

Pray for the spirit of forgiveness. Call on God to do the heavy lifting; because His grace is necessary to reduce and eventually destroy this passion of anger. You can see that a careful analysis of the cause of any problem is also necessary if you hope to rid yourself of it. Like any form of weakness, there's a need to persevere in the healing process.

Morality should be an essential part of everyone's education. The Church is often criticized for insisting on this discipline by always stressing the danger of sin, but secular society claims the right to punish criminals, thieves, and those who do harm to others. To neglect a child's moral training can lead to all kinds of trouble.

The opioid epidemic, which killed over 100,000 people in the last couple of years in the U.S. alone is a preventable disease. Wise parents realize they need help in the moral education of their children and the Catholic School system wants to help them. It's a win-win situation.

May the Lord be your strength and your joy as you carry out the responsibility.

COPING WITH LIFE

By Fr. John T. Catoir, JCD | July 21, 2017

In today's political climate, there are a lot of people on both sides of the aisle who have become emotionally upset by the 2016 elections. I won't go into the politics of it, but I thought it might be helpful to discuss the flood of toxic emotions that many are experiencing.

We know that sadness, fear, and anger will gradually sap our energy and lead to exhaustion. So let's concentrate on the thoughts that lead to feelings of happiness and joy.

We're all trying to improve our mental health. To succeed, we need to rid ourselves of toxic thinking. Our emotions all flow from the thoughts we allow ourselves to think. We are seeking peace of soul.

Happiness is the by-product of a meaningful life. The senses play a part in this. We are delighted by a delicious meal; we take comfort wearing warm clothes on a chilly day. The smell of fresh seaside air lifts our mood.

Joy, on the other hand, emerges from deep within the soul. Joy is the state of peace that comes from being in harmony with God's will. The sight of a majestic sunset makes us grateful to God for the gift of beauty. The birth of a baby brings us to our knees with tears of gratitude.

St. Augustine said, "Our hearts are restless until they rest in Thee, O Lord." This rest may seem like a distant goal, but the truth is you can find it in The Lord anytime you choose. You can take a moment to ask Him for the spiritual rest you need.

The first step is to stop your frantic thinking. Listen to your breathing. Reflect on God's love within you. The joy that will follow is the simplest form of gratitude.

Escaping from the toxic thinking that weighs you down is the first step to attaining happiness and joy. It's a matter of being in touch with God's Joy. Prayer will open your receptivity to the gift of Divine Joy.

You may not be a saint, but there's no need to be discouraged. Even if you're not perfect, you ARE loved by God and therefore a saint-in-training.

The virtue of hope comes into play. If you hope for better days, you will not be disappointed. The Lord says, "In this world you will have troubles," but "take heart—be of good cheer—for I have overcome the world." (John 16:33).

Knowing that better days are coming will enable you to turn away from the rat race and focus more on joy. Joy transcends the noise of the world. The state of spiritual gladness will soon purify your former mental swamp and you will feel God's peace.

It will take an act of the will to stop sabotaging your mind with toxic thoughts, but your chances of attaining greater peace and joy will increase rapidly as soon as you make the decision to live joyfully.

The Lord is always there to keep you afloat. By controlling your negative thinking, you will be able to feel God's joy pulsing though your soul.

Supernatural joy is the most wonderful gift you will ever receive, and it's yours for the asking.

COURAGE AND COWARDICE

By Fr. John T. Catoir, JCD | June 8, 2012

"The virtue more admired in a person than any other is courage. Courage has many names including: endurance, patience, loyalty, consistency with the truth, and a willingness to face whatever comes before you."

– Archbishop Alban Goodier, S.J.

The word virtue, or 'virtus' in Latin, means 'power'. Courage is the power to stand fast and live through hardship in the performance of one's duty. During the years that I was the Director of Eva's Village, a drug and alcohol rehab in the City of Paterson, New Jersey, I learned a great deal about the courage of recovering addicts. I experienced the struggle men and woman faced as they fought to take their lives back.

We define things more precisely by negative iteration. For instance, the opposite of courage is cowardice. Everyone knows it's far easier to shirk responsibility than to persevere courageously. We know that there is a price that must be paid for bravery. Those who give up and run-away display cowardice.

I don't have to tell you what it means to have your self-respect or what it means to lose it. A person who does wrong allows the shame to become part of his or her life. Self-respect is a key ingredient of happiness. The addict secretly carries a heavy burden. Maybe it's caused by an addiction to drugs or alcohol or sexuality, or a combination all three.

The easy way out is to deny you have a problem, but this only leads to living a double life. It begins to eat away at your confidence. Unless you face up to the harm you are doing to yourself and those who love you, you'll never find the courage to escape from it. Finding your way back to the truth takes guts. "I must beat this; I'm killing myself slowly." It takes extraordinary courage to break the deadly cycle of addiction and go for help.

We are all human. We all feel pity for ourselves at times, but self-pity is a sure way of remaining helpless. Straight talk is needed. We must be truthful and tell it like it is. We know that millions of men and women have bravely gone through the 12-Step Program and endured rehab therapy. They have won the battle and won their lives back. Their self-respect returned. It has been done by millions of courageous men and women.

Here's another quote from Archbishop Goodier, "Jesus singles out the blind and says, "Father, forgive them for they know not what they do." For the weak, Jesus holds out a helping hand. He treated Judas with compassion to the very end. But when they hid their problem under the garb of brazenness, when they sinned and taught others to sin, He had only indignation. He leaves them to their self-inflicted sentences until they repent."

To find the courage to free yourself from this living hell takes determination, prayer, and trust in God's love. Repent and make amends. With God's help you can do all things. You can claim the power to become a person of great courage.

Don't accept the lie that you can't live without your drug of choice. Don't carry on with arrogance. Don't be a coward because it will only lead to a coward's doom.

This proverb can be of help, "If at first you don't succeed, try, try again". Hope works wonders.

May the Lord be your strength and your joy.

CREATE YOUR OWN FUTURE
By Fr. John T. Catoir, JCD | November 10, 2019

"All the way to heaven is heaven." – St. Catherine of Siena

We gradually become what we think about. The thoughts we dwell on enable us to become what we want to be. They have the power to transform us into extraordinary human beings. This is good news for saints-in-training.

Most of us think worthy thoughts most of the time. Sometimes fear and toxic thoughts barge in uninvited. In moments of exhaustion or sadness we become vulnerable. No one is perfect.

Not to worry; you are not your thoughts. You are the observer of your thoughts. More precisely, you are the editor of your thoughts. Delete the dark ones, affirm the light ones, and your life will be a lot happier.

Jesus is the Light that comes into the darkness. When you feel like you're in a dark tunnel, instantly change the channel. Imagine yourself in heaven at the beach having an adult beverage with the Lord. Life will be a lot easier if you manage your thoughts with a sense of humor.

"Don't be afraid," said the Lord. Those words appear 365 times in the Bible. It means that you have the power to banish needless anxiety. Jesus would never have uttered them if they were not true. You have the power to reject fear. You can imagine yourself as Joan of Arc or the Angel Gabriel.

On a more intellectual note, the following ideas may be of help. They are taken from Dr. Abraham Low, M.D., the psychiatrist who wrote, *Mental Health Through Will Training:* "The will plays a crucial role in controlling your thoughts. It is vital that you reject upsetting thoughts."

The will is the center of the personality. St. Thomas Aquinas and Dr. Low agree on this point. It is a belief that is very much in harmony with Catholic thinking. The key is in the word: habitual. Make a habit of collecting uplifting ideas. Write them down. You can control your emotions better by controlling the thoughts you allow yourself to think.

You are responsible for your own actions. You know the courts will send you to prison if you commit a crime. Therefore, you must reject any thoughts or temptations that will lead to criminal behavior. And if you want to go further and become a saint, press the same reject button for thoughts that can lead to immoral activities.

Multiple addictions can develop in the life of a good person if he or she has no long-range plan. Therefore, plan for the attainment of salvation. If you feel weak at times, don't be discouraged. Be like St. Paul who boasted of his weakness, "For when I am weak, then I call on Christ to make me strong." With prayer and determination, you can do this.

If you're already suffering from an addiction, check out the Third Step: "Turn my life and my will over to the God of my understanding." For Christians, that would be Jesus. Millions of alcoholics, druggies, gamblers, overeaters and sexaholics have found salvation and sobriety through the 12 Step Program. Turning control over to the Lord takes great faith, but it works.

Either way, you can control your thoughts, your feelings and your actions. Suicidal thoughts be damned. Replace them with the thought that God wants you to make others happy, not miserable. Set a good example and be brave.

May the Lord be your strength and your joy.

C.S. LEWIS: WHY BE CATHOLIC?

By Fr. John T. Catoir, JCD | April 29, 2019

We seldom see the hidden hand of God at work in this world, but God is always active in human history. C.S. Lewis always stressed the fact that, "The Church will outlive the universe, and because of this, the individual person within it will outlive the universe." I've been asked to repeat this column, and here it is with few improvements...

Everything that is joined to the immortal head of the

C. S. Lewis (Source: Alamy Photo)

Mystical Body of Christ will share his immortality. Lewis insisted that if we do not believe this truth "we might as relegate the Christian faith to the museums." Neither individuals nor communities can inherit eternal life unless they belong to the Mystical Body of Christ. The secular world is blind to this truth.

Lewis debunked the un-Christian notion that each one of us starts with the treasure we call the "personality" locked up within us, and life is about becoming famous. He scoffed, "But no one who seeks fame or originality for its own sake will ever become either famous or original."

Considering the truths of the Gospel, we know that the true goal of human life is to abide in Jesus Christ and attain heaven. We are called to tell the truth as we see it, doing our job as well as it can be done for the work's sake. When we succeed at this, originality and sometimes fame will come unsought. Only in Him and with Him and through Him will the goal of eternal life become possible.

The time will come when every culture, every institution, every nation, and the entire human race including every biological life form in this world will become extinct. The solar system and the billions of galaxies in outer space will all burn themselves out and disappear. Nothing is eternal but God, and those who share his life.

Immortality, which is the gift of living beyond the limits of this world, will only come to those who belong to the inner life of God. This gift is bestowed on us by virtue of our membership in Christ's Body. By belonging to his Mystical Body we come to share in His eternal destiny.

Lewis maintained, "Our immortality is directly related to our union with Christ. Baptism makes us an organic part of the Body of Christ. The Mystical Body of Christ is a metaphor for the cosmic Christ, who pervades and penetrates the entire universe." Metaphors help us to explain the unexplainable, which is the very purpose of all theology.

"Therein lies the maddening ambiguity of our faith as it appears to others. As private individuals, as mere biological entities, each with a separate existence, we all appear to be of little account but as members of the Body of Christ, we are assured of our eternal self-identity and shall live to remember the galaxies as an old tale."

The Catholic Catechism defines membership in the Mystical Body of Christ as extending beyond the membership of the Roman Catholic Church. Then who are the members? All who sincerely call Jesus the Lord of their lives are certainly members, and Jesus established the Catholic Church to bring us all home. Exactly how? That is something hidden from our eyes.

Why be Catholic? Everyone must answer that for themselves.

DEMENTIA AND SPIRITUALITY
By Fr. John T. Catoir, JCD | January 30, 2018

This interesting request came to me from one of my readers, "I would like to get another copy of your book, *Enjoy the Lord*. My mother has dementia and misplaced her copy…I remember her telling me how much she loved that book."

I was happy to oblige. It's well known that many people who are cognitively impaired are intensely aware of God's presence. How so? There is an inner faculty in each one us called the soul. It functions in ways we do not fully understand.

I remember reading a story by Victor Frankl, the psychoanalyst who survived the death camps of Auschwitz. In his book, *Man's Search for Meaning*, he tells of a young Jewish woman who was in a world of her own, and yet was happy chanting Jewish hymns.

Many people who are losing their grip on life report that they find solace in thinking about the love of God. My book must have brought comfort to this woman because it was in plain English, not written in theological jargon or psychobabble.

If you're at a point where you think you need a shrink, remember that he or she will be asking: "what is it that you really want?" I like to ask, "What is it that God wants of you?"

In some cases, the pursuit of what you want is the very thing that brought you to a state of discomfort. Our souls are restless until they rest in God and our happiness is bound up with Him. Above all, believe in God's forgiveness.

Prayer is helpful in this endeavor. Going back to the Psalms we find a key concept: "I place my trust in Thee, O God. My life is in your hands." (Psalm 31:15) Prayer and the proper medication can work wonders.

If you are suffering from emotional or mental difficulties, don't despair. We know a great deal more about chemical imbalance today than ever before. Medical therapy is now far advanced and finding the right balance of medication can produce amazing results.

Have you ever heard of St. Dymphna, the patron Saint of those afflicted with nervous and mental disorders? She was the only daughter of a pagan King named Damon who ruled over the Oriel region of Ireland back in the 7th Century.

When Dymphna was fourteen, her mother died and afterward, King Damon went slightly mad. He demanded that Dymphna marry him. She was terrified and absolutely refused. Soon she ran away and was safe for a time. The King found her, they argued, and in a state of rage he drew his sword, and struck off his daughter's head.

According to tradition, many people with epilepsy and mental illness who visited her tomb were cured. Her feast day is May 15th and many healings are still being reported.

Whether you rely on modern medicine or the intercession of the saints, stay calm. Mental illness is not fatal. Many who were once in deep trouble are now healed and happy.

May the Lord be your strength and your joy.

DIVINE MERCY

By Fr. John T. Catoir, JCD | April 8, 2018

The message of Divine Mercy is simple. It is that God loves us, all of us. And He wants us to recognize that His mercy is greater than our sins so that we can call upon Him with trust and receive His forgiveness.

What else do you know about Divine Mercy? Read on for my take on this mystery. I discovered something I never thought about before. Namely, that all the saints we pray to and admire were once mediocre sinners, every one of them.

On the Sunday right after Easter, the Church reminds us of the sins of the Apostles. We celebrate Divine Mercy Sunday because God forgave those closest to Him – the Apostles – who ran away in fear for their lives after the crucifixion. He did so much to prepare them, and yet they turned out to be cowards when He needed them most.

The Gospel centered on Doubting Thomas who refused to believe that Jesus was risen even after the others testified that they had seen Him. "Until I see the nail marks in his hands and put my finger where the nails were…I will not believe!" (John 20:25) These are the words of a defiant man still too frightened to trust his friends.

The reason this Sunday is called Divine Mercy Sunday is because it points to the fact that the Apostles, who later became saints and martyrs, were once spiritual pipsqueaks and unrepentant hypocrites. Their excuses are understandable, but their performance under fire was unworthy of them.

I'll bet there were times in your life when you thought of yourself as far from perfect, to say the least. Divine Mercy Sunday sends the message that all the saints and martyrs who ever lived were once mediocre, flawed human beings.

Only by the mercy of God were they restored to the state of grace and enabled to fulfill their destiny in life. It is a message of hope. The supernatural virtue of hope is defined as "expectation with certainty." You can rely on God's mercy and forgiveness.

A deeper understanding of the meaning of forgiveness can help you to fully appreciate this mystery. Forgiveness reconciles your mind and heart with God, with neighbor, and most of all with self.

"The forgiven penitent is reconciled with himself in his inmost being, where he regains his own true identity. He is reconciled with his brethren, whom he has in some way wounded, and he is reconciled with the Church, and with all creation." – Pope John Paul II

The Lord stands ready to forgive everyone, including you. You in turn must be ready to forgive others and yourself. "Forgive us our trespasses as we forgive those who trespass against us."

I leave you with this prayer written by Cardinal John Henry Newman: "God created me to do Him some definite service. He has committed some work to me which He has not committed to another. I have a mission. I am a link in a chain, a bond of connection between persons. Therefore, I will trust Him. If I am sick, my sickness may serve Him, in perplexity, my perplexity may serve Him. If I am in sorrow, my sorrow may serve Him. He does nothing in vain. He knows what He's about."

DO YOU HEAR THE VOICE OF LOVE?
By Fr. John T. Catoir, JCD | March 8, 2018

Faith hears the voice of love speaking and abiding in one's heart. It pervades and penetrates one's whole being.

God is always acting in our lives. He usually speaks ever so softly. The message is simple, "I have come that your joy may be full." He wants you to know that you can face the hardships of life and still find contentment. The knowledge of God's love will sustain you. He wants you to be appreciative of the fact that He is supplying you with hope, inspiration, strength, and encouragement.

Coping with the miseries of life can be challenging. If you've had a parent who wasn't there for you when you were in need, you know what it is to be miserable and emotionally drained. Nevertheless, God wants you to recover and move forward. He speaks to you. From the deep recesses of your mind the Lord whispers, "Be happy anyway."

Perhaps you've experienced betrayal by a trusted friend, someone who was caught stealing from you. You were furious at first and it turned to hurt. Then you hear that inner voice saying, "Be happy anyway." Jesus came to earth that your joy may be full and He speaks to you frequently about it.

Life is shattered time and again by broken hearts, unexpected deaths, and spiteful neighbors. Sometimes your own human weakness brings added misery. Through it all, faith hears the voice of love speaking a language that seems foreign to our ears.

When we try to understand how God thinks, we look to Jesus for guidance. And what do we find? At the heart of God's great love for us we find The Way of the Cross. "For this you have been called, because Christ suffered for you, leaving an example, so that you should follow in His steps."(1 Peter 2:21)

Christ's passion and death show us true love. Jesus is the way. "No one has greater love than this, than to lay down one's life out of love for His friends." (John 15-13)

The passion of Christ was a Spiritual demonstration of how we are called to live our lives in self-giving, without counting the cost.

"The memory of the Passion of Jesus is the door which leads to intimate union with God." – St. Paul of the Cross.

By depending on God's strength and joy, we gain victory over death and joy gradually prevails over sorrow. By serving God and neighbor as best we can, we suffer many crosses but joy soon follows. We hear the faint words of God, "Be happy anyway."

How is it possible to recover from abandonment, betrayal, or the death of a loved one? In the natural order it isn't, but by listening to our inner voice, we gain perspective. All the miseries that surrounds us gradually lose their power. We begin to pay them no mind. We only listen to the words:

"Be happy anyway, my chosen one, holy and beloved; clothe yourself with compassion, kindness, humility, meekness, and patience, and all will be well." (Colossians 3:12)

May the Lord be your strength and your joy.

DON'T WORRY, BE HAPPY

By Fr. John T. Catoir, JCD | September 23, 2018

With Hurricane Florence, the Tariff Wars, and life in general, we've all had a lot to worry about in the past few months. I thought a return to the wisdom of singer Bobby McFerrin might be of help. Remember his little ditty from 1989? "Don't worry, be happy. Every life will have some trouble, but when you worry you make it double."

Is this kind of advice unrealistic or is it a reasonable form of folk wisdom? After all, there is a grain of truth in it. By focusing on our fears we put them on center stage and keep looking at them. Focus on God's love more. We can take the words of Jesus seriously when He says, "Be not anxious." Therefore, focus more on the words of Jesus. Even though we may not be able to control our fears completely, we can control our thinking. The thoughts we allow ourselves to think have a powerful influence on the way we feel.

For instance, when we think we're in danger, we feel dread and anguish. But when we think there is no danger we feel safe and sound. If a child is reassured that there is no monster lurking under the bed, she is reassured and can safely go to sleep. The way you decide to look at life matters. Admittedly, there are times when serious anguish takes over and fear becomes terribly distressing. When a spouse is dying, or a child is hooked on drugs, or a romance is breaking apart, words seldom bring relief. Sometimes even the words of Jesus cannot penetrate the depth of a person's sorrow.

Often we turn to our faith in God as our last resort. God is the last great hope of the human spirit. We turn to prayer because we know instinctively that prayer has worked wonders in the lives of untold millions. St. Paul urged us to pray without ceasing. How is that possible? St. Augustine has some much-needed wisdom to help us answer that question: "The constancy of your desire (for a cure, or a restoration of peace, etc.) will itself be the ceaseless voice of your prayer. Your worry itself takes the form of prayer. The desires of your heart, all become your ceaseless prayer before the face of a merciful God, who listens to His beloved children with love."

So from St. Augustine's perspective, worry isn't a terrible thing at all, nor a waste. He's telling us that worry is a human, normal part of life. True, we all need relief from unrelenting fear and suffering, but we still have the power to smile through it all, and even to forgive ourselves for not trusting enough.

If a song like: "Don't Worry, Be Happy" helps you diffuse the pain, then sing it often. If the anxiety persists, decide to be happy anyway. Make believe your prayer is being answered. Time heals all wounds, and this too will pass. Believe that you have a good chance of having your ceaseless prayers answered by your merciful Father. But in the meantime, carry your cross with courage. Be like Christ, who humbly submitted to His cross. Be assured that He will give you the strength to bear it.

May the Lord not only be your strength, but also your joy as you persevere through the trials and tribulations of life.

DUNKIRK

By Fr. John T. Catoir, JCD | August 8, 2017

The movie "Dunkirk" is drawing large crowds as it tells the amazing story of the World War II sea rescue of 338,000 British soldiers trapped on the beaches of northern France. Eight hundred privately owned yachts and boats crossed the English Channel under constant enemy fire to save their fellow countrymen.

What the movie did not portray was the plight of the civilian refugees in the town of Dunkirk itself. The German Army's advance created a refugee crisis of major proportions. Over a thousand civilians died from the merciless bombing at Dunkirk.

A first-hand account of those tragic days was written by my friend Catherine deVinck. Here is an excerpt:

> "On May 10, 1940, the German Army invaded Belgium, my native country. I was eighteen years old, living in Brussels with my grandfather, mother, and my sixteen-year old brother. My father, a Major in the Belgian Army, was away with his troops.
>
> "I was awakened that fateful morning by the sound of German bombers flying over the city, and by the explosions of bombs thundering in the distance. Filled with fear, my mother decided we had to flee the city to get as far away from Hitler's army as possible.
>
> "Many thousands flooded the roads making the evacuation a nightmare. When we finally got to the train station it was mobbed, but we managed to squeeze on board. At the next stop we found another bus, and finally arrived at Dunkirk. We thought we'd be among the first, but the streets were already filled with refugees. There was no lodging to be found anywhere. Entire families were bedded down in the streets, and we followed suit.
>
> "We knew we had to leave Dunkirk as soon as possible to find lodging. The next morning my mother learned there was a bus leaving from the main square where hundreds were waiting to get on board.

"The crowd parted when the bus arrived, and by chance it stopped right next to us. However, when the crowd surged forward, I was thrown under the bus before it came to a complete stop.

"My mother screamed as the huge rear wheel came to rest against my left thigh. I fainted. I wasn't hurt, but part of my skirt was still under the wheel. In a state of shock, I felt the people pulling me and my skirt free. As a result, the bus driver let us get on the bus first.

"The near fatal accident turned out to be a blessing in disguise. Eventually, we made our way to the southwest coast of France, near Spain. We found lodging, and thanks be to God, managed to survive.

"When the war ended, we were all reunited in Brussels. I met my husband José and we had many children, grandchildren, and great-grandchildren. I can still see the despair and fear on the faces of the families that flooded Dunkirk with us.

"I am 95 now, and I pray often for the victims of war. I often wonder what became of the Dunkirk survivors."

It has been my pleasure to know the deVinck family for fifty years. Catherine's husband José, a Belgian baron, died last year at age 100. He and I co-authored a book entitled, "The Challenge of Love." José served in the Belgian army under Catherine's father who was promoted to the rank of General toward the end of the war. It was he who introduced his daughter Catherine to José.

EASTER 2018

By Fr. John T. Catoir, JCD | February 26, 2018

Happy Easter. If you've been reading my columns over the years, you know that I return time and again to my favorite scripture quotes. Let's unpack them together and see what the Lord has in store for us today.

Don't think that the Feast of the Resurrection is a seasonal celebration. St. Paul said, "Rejoice always and in all circumstances! Give thanks to the Lord, for this is the will of God for you in Christ Jesus." (1 Thessalonians 5:16)

Because Jesus rose from the dead, "We are an Easter people and Alleluia is our song."– St. Augustine.

The call to joy is intended to last from here to eternity. You may not feel joyous every day, but with the help of God you can learn to cope better with life; improving day by day. To begin the process, start taking Jesus at his word.

"Look at the birds in the sky; they do not sow or reap, they gather nothing into barns, yet your heavenly Father feeds them. Are you not more important than they?" (Matthew 6:26).

Yes, of course you are! Trust the Lord and listen to His advice. Put your ego aside and become childlike. Literally, "Look at the birds in the sky." They live in the present moment. They are unselfconscious and seemingly carefree. Use nature to remind you of your supernatural calling; namely, to love God with your whole heart.

Bring the Lord with you wherever you go. Be a blessing for everyone you meet. Accept God's' love with gladness, and always remember: you and God are intimately united.

"I am the vine, you are the branches; he who abides in Me and Me in him, is the one who bears much fruit; for without Me you can do nothing." (John 15:1-5)

Since the life of God is blissful and beatified, your life will be bathed in His light. There is a kind of spiritual osmosis that is taking place all time.

"In Him, you live and breathe and have your being." (Acts 17:28)

In the state of nature, we live with aches and pains, having good days and bad, but by faith we live in the Lord. We have become a new creation. Can't you feel it? Yes, you can! Put aside all doubt, the truth will set you free.

On the cross Jesus said, "It is consummated." Mission accomplished! He came to earth that your joy may be complete. Do you ever doubt it, or wonder if He accomplished this miracle for you, in your corner of the world? Pierre Teilhard de Chardin never doubted. He used these words to express his Joy:

"It is done. The Fire has penetrated the earth…All things individually and collectively are penetrated and flooded by Divine energy. Jesus is the connecting link in the unity of the cosmos."

"Let the hearts of those who seek the Lord, rejoice!" (1 Chronicles 16:10)

Faith hears the voice of love speaking, dwelling within one's heart, pervading and permeating one's whole being.

"For God so loved the world, that He gave His only Son, so that everyone who believes in Him may have eternal life." (John 3:16)

EVOLUTION REVISITED

By Fr. John T. Catoir, JCD | June 13, 2019

Darwin's theory of evolution has prompted many Catholics to question their faith. Before you make the same mistake, you should know more about the troubles that surround Darwin's theory. Many aspects of evolution are disputed even among his own followers. They are divided into two main groups: The Gradualists and the Saltationists.

The Gradualists maintain that the higher species of life evolved gradually from the lower forms of life by small changes over millions of years. This process of Darwin is called "natural selection."

The Saltationists say there is no scientific evidence to prove Darwin's theory of Gradualism. The Saltationists maintain that new forms of life do appear, but only suddenly, after millions of years of stability. They believe that a reptile one day produced an egg that one day produced, not a reptile, but a bird. They claim this was all done without any Divine intervention, which was the main purpose of the testing: to prove there was no God.

Scholar Larry Azar responded, "If any sane person believes this, then surely he must believe in fairy tales." Azar wrote a 619-page book with 42 pages of carefully researched scientific bibliography entitled, *Evolution and Other Fairy Tales* (published by Author House, Bloomington, Indiana, July 2005). It is a book which carefully studies the claims of the evolutionists and examines the logic and cogency of their arguments.

Popes John Paul II and Benedict XVI only approved the concept of Theistic Evolution, which presumes that God is the first cause of our evolving universe. How and when we humans appeared in this process is not spelled out clearly.

Fr. Kenneth Baker, S.J., wrote an excellent review of Azar's book in *Homilectic & Pastoral Magazine*, July 2006, saying "This is not a book of creation science. It is a critical analysis of the claims of the evolutionists. Fr. Baker shows that there is no evidence whatsoever for evolution, in the sense that essential changes occur in a rising spiral from the amoeba, to reptiles, to birds, to mammals, to apes, to man."

In other words, no proof of evolution from species to species.

Beware all you Catholics who left your religion behind because of your misguided acceptance of the unverifiable theory of evolution. You have traded your birthright for a myth.

Einstein is correct, " There must be a supreme intelligence behind the universe." The Church is also correct in teaching that Jesus Christ is our divine Savior. The story of the fall in Genesis is not to be interpreted as literal history; rather it is a revealed truth that teaches us to turn to Jesus as our Lord and Savior.

For me the doctrine of original sin proclaims the fallen state of mankind and is the easiest doctrine to prove. Just look at the carnage of the last Century. The theory of evolution gave Nazi Germany and Marxist Communism the principle of racial superiority, which many used to validate their belief that certain classes of people, such as Jews, Gypsies, Negroes and Catholics, were inferior to the Germanic Race. It is a theory that is deeply flawed.

Jesus said, "By their fruits you will know them."

FEAR IS THE ENEMY

By Fr. John T. Catoir, JCD | 1970s

Have you ever suffered from a morbid dissatisfaction with your daily life, or been haunted by the feeling that the years are slipping by too fast and you're not becoming the person you always wanted to be?

Chances are you need a retreat or a day of recollection, or maybe as little as two hours alone in your thoughts. Robert Louis Stevenson once wrote, "Most of us lead lives that two hours of reflection would lead us to disown."

Source: momentsofwords.blogspot.com

I'm not sure I completely agree with Stevenson. Most of us are on the right track, living the life God has called us to live but our mental attitude is often burdened by needless worry and an unfortunate propensity to put ourselves down.

Three areas of difficulty that need to be examined to break out of the doldrums are: 1) the degree of one's inner censorship; 2) the extent of one's feelings of inferiority; and 3) the quality of one's kindness to others.

Taking the third point first: it goes without saying that the more you think of others, the less you will be preoccupied with yourself. Thinking of others will force you to cling to God more because it isn't always easy to be a loving person. Draw power from Him every day and your charitable nature will blossom like spring flowers.

Regarding point one: if you are worn out by your own inner censorship, it is probably a throw-back to your upbringing. The severe voice of a censoring parent has a way of remaining in the psyche. The trick is to learn to forgive yourself frequently and laugh at yourself more. God loves you and forgives you, so why act as though you are outside of his saving grace? Wake up!

And point two: Feelings of inferiority are a more complex emotional problem to deal with. If you have the habit of putting yourself down by always underrating your abilities, try to change your thinking patterns. Fear is the enemy. Fear of criticism, fear of punishment, and fear of failure will get you nowhere. Distance yourself from fear. The child in you is afraid, but you are an adult.

Take that frightened child by the hand and ignore all screams of resistance. Go out and meet the challenges of the day. You are under the Lord's blessing, so no matter what happens, cling to the knowledge of His love. God's life is in you. Can you imagine what that means? Lift your heart and have a new confidence.

FINDING PEACE

By Fr. John T. Catoir, JCD | 1970s

In my book *Enjoy the Lord,* I proclaimed the beauty of God's unchanging love. St. Augustine (354–430 AD) expressed the same idea 1,500 years ago. Here's a little exercise recommended:

"Think back to one of the great and happy moments of our life, a time when you were in the bloom of health. Do you have it in mind? Imagine that moment going on and on, leaving behind all other sights and

St Augustine by artist Sandro Botticelli.
(Source: Wikipedia)

sounds. You have only this vision to ravish and absorb you in a spirit of joy. Imagine that the rest of your eternal life would be like that moment of illumination which leaves you breathless."

In this meditation, St. Augustine suggests that it is possible to begin to approximate the joys of heaven right now. We are destined for an eternity of happiness, so let us begin our journey toward the light right now.

Times change, the body grows old, people come and go, but your soul lives on forever. It is necessary at times to discern the presence of God abiding within you. The knowledge of God's love spurs you on to pray that wordless prayer called contemplation. Contemplation is the art of enjoying the Lord.

St. Teresa of Avila referred to it as the Prayer of Quiet, the art of connecting one's mind, one's body and, most importantly, one's will to the universal will of God. Here is what she wrote:

"We cannot, in spite of all our efforts, procure this by ourselves. It is a form of peace in which the soul establishes herself or rather in which God establishes the soul. All her powers are at rest. She understands but not by senses that she is already near her God, and if she draws a little nearer, she will become one with Him, feeling great bodily comfort and a great satisfaction of the soul. Such is the happiness of the soul so close to the spring that even without drinking of the waters she finds herself refreshed."

St. Augustine also wrote about enjoying the Lord through contemplative prayer. He said it was like being lifted beyond ourselves into a Godly state of peace. "Far be it from me, O Lord, to think I am happy for any or every joy that I may remember. For there is a joy which is given to those who love Thee for Thy own sake, and this joy is Thyself." In Augustine's thinking, true joy is an awareness of the hidden radiance of God shining within us. It transcends even the happiest of earthly memories. Ultimately, we realize that the highest joy is God's gift of Himself.

St. Teresa offers her own reflections on the spiritual ascent: "Indeed, to those who are in this state it seems that you are no longer in this world." Both Teresa and Augustine acknowledge that these brief moments of rapture come and go, but they give us a glimpse of the sweetness of the life to come.

If you feel yourself getting caught up in the frenzy of Christmas, why not put a few minutes aside each day and enter into the Prayer of Quiet. Absorb God's love. Be still and know that God is closer to you than your own heartbeat. When you return to your daily routine, the aftertaste of this delightful visit will keep you in a state of peace and bring joy to your heart.

GOOD FRIDAY
By Fr. John T. Catoir, JCD | February 18, 2018

On Thursday evening, Jesus retreated from the upper room and went to a nearby garden to pray. An agonizing emotion came over Him as He awaited His fate. After an hour or so, He heard men talking in the distance. He looked up and there was Judas leading a group of soldiers. They came toward Him and Judas betrayed Jesus with a kiss. The soldiers arrested Him immediately and brought Him before Pilate. He was falsely accused and condemned to be tortured.

For an hour Jesus was beaten, scourged, and crowned with thorns. Pilate heard the mob shouting: "Crucify Him! Crucify Him!," and he condemned Jesus to death by crucifixion.

On the way up the hill to Golgotha, 'The Place of the Skull', where all public crucifixions were held, Jesus fell twice. The mob cursed Him all along the way. His mother Mary followed in anguish. Seeing her in such obvious pain only added to His own sorrow. When Jesus fell a third time, a stranger named Simon was pulled out of the crowd. The soldiers made him help Jesus continue up the hill.

A woman named Veronica suddenly appeared from the crowd to wipe Our Lord's blood-soaked face. He was able to see a group of women keening in tears. He told them not to weep for Him, but for themselves and their children. All this time Jesus felt the wood of the cross scraping against the open wounds on His back. He was losing blood rapidly.

When they reached the place where He was to be crucified, the soldiers stripped Him of his garments and jeered at Him. He humbly submitted to their brutality. A soldier threw Him to the ground. His crown of thorns hit the cross and dug in more deeply. Once again, His face was covered with blood. A soldier held His outstretched arm down and hammered a six-inch spike into the wrist of Jesus, fastening Him to the cross. This same excruciating procedure was repeated with His other arm.

They lifted the whole structure and dropped it into a hole. Jesus screamed in agony. Hanging between two thieves, He cried out in a loud voice, "My God, my God, why have You forsaken me?" (Matthew 27:45).

As God incarnate, Jesus was in constant union with His Father's love, but He was suffering from extreme shock and was near death. He hung from the cross struggling for breath, as they pierced His side with a sword. Jesus breathed his last breath,

"It is consummated."

The crowd became silent. Suddenly the earth shook and a great darkness came over the land. The people were terrified. One soldier was heard to say, "This man truly was the Son of God." (Matthew 27:54)

Peter and the other disciples had scattered out of fear for their lives but a wealthy disciple, Joseph of Arimathea, came forward. He had already asked permission from Pilate to take down the lifeless body of Jesus and prepare it for burial. Mary was there at the foot of the cross; she held Him on her lap and wept.

Once Jesus was laid in Joseph's tomb, the soldiers sealed it closed with a huge rock. Two soldiers stood guard at the tomb throughout the night.

The passion and death of Jesus had come to an end. What happened next was the miracle of miracles.

On the third day, Jesus rose from the dead.

GOD LOVES YOU
By Fr. John T. Catoir, JCD | July 15, 2018

How amazing is this? God loves you! The unity between the New and Old Testaments of the Bible on this single idea is mind-boggling. Let's go back 2,700 years or so. I want you to meet the prophet Zephaniah. He lived around 650 B.C. In his day, the people worshiped inanimate objects: the stars, the moon and the sun, but Zephaniah came along and had the gall to denounce their pagan practices. He preached a series of ideas held sacred by the Jews. These ideas formed the basis of the Judeo-Christian tradition; namely, that there is only one God and He is essentially a God of Love.

To the ears of most who were living at the time, this was preposterous! But to those who embraced this personal understanding of God, Zephaniah promised the fullness of joy. He ended his book with a hymn of joy which was sung jubilantly for centuries by faithful Jews all over the world. The passage I like best from Zephaniah's work is found in Chapter 3:17. It speaks poetically about God's love: "God will exult with joy over you...He will renew you by his love. He will dance with shouts of joy over you, as on a day of festival." (Cf. the Jerusalem Bible)

One of the first signs of God's love is His very desire to be loved by His people. He wants them to love Him back. He promotes public worship. He inspired the psalmist to pray, "My soul longs for you, O God." (Psalm 42:2)

Pope Benedict XVI wrote about the mystery of Divine Love. "I want my first Encyclical – *God is Love* – to speak of the love God lavishes upon us." The pope almost writes it as a romance where God tries to woo us into leaving behind everything that is counterproductive to our union with Him. His strategy is very subtle. He never tampers with our freedom. Love is a free gift and He wants us to love Him with our free will. He gives us the power to please Him.

God could have easily overpowered us with His divine attributes, but that would have put us in a kind of bondage to Him. We would all end up as His love-slaves. No, He wants us to give ourselves freely.

Pope Benedict made the connection between an egotistical life (one that is self-absorbed) and a life that is centered in God. "Authentic self-discovery…is a journey, and an ongoing exodus out of the closed, inward looking self." He then draws an interesting conclusion: "Whoever seeks to gain his life will lose it, but whoever loses his life for my sake, will preserve it." (Luke 17:33)

The message is clear: only those who live by faith can learn to be dependent on the Lord and thereby grow in union with Him. "God so loved the world, He gave His only begotten Son so that everyone who believes in Him…may have eternal life." (John 3:16)

Cast off any doubts you may have about your chances of winning God's love. He loved you long before you were born. He has given you the gift of life because He has a deep and abiding love for you.

HAPPINESS: OUR DESTINY
By Fr. John T. Catoir, JCD | 1970s

According to St Bernard of Clairvaux, "The whole of the spiritual life consists of two elements. When we think of ourselves, we are perturbed and filled with salutary sadness. And when we think of the Lord, we are revived, finding consolation in the joy of the Holy Spirit. From the first, we derive fear and humility. From the second, hope and love.

Since thinking about the Lord and his promise of eternal life is the highest element of the spiritual life, what would happen to you if you decided to concentrate more on the Lord and less on yourself? Would it fill your soul with hope as St. Bernard suggests? And would it enable you to share your joyful spirit with others? St. Bernard seems to think so, and for what it's worth, so do I.

If each one of us would try to become a more joyful person in our personal lives, this would be a happier world. Wouldn't it be wonderful if we were able to put Jesus first in all things? I think it would cause a monumental change for the better.

You've heard it said that one person can make a difference. It's true. Even a little pebble when thrown in a pond can make ripples. Psychologists tell us that one person affects the lives of at least eight others for better or worse, and each of them will affect the lives of eight more. In other words, we touch many lives and change them for better or worse.

Like a snowflake, you are beautiful, fragile and utterly unique. But unlike a snowflake, you have eternal life. The Lord God wanted you to be born and He plans an eternity of happiness for you.

This is our faith, and each of us is called to respond to this Good News with enthusiasm. So what would happen if you decided to claim your birthright by choosing to be happy because of the knowledge of God's love? Since happiness is God's will for you anyway, why wait until you're in heaven? Happiness is your destiny.

I'm not speaking here about narcissism, that inordinate love of self which leads to selfish indulgence. Just the opposite. I'm speaking about abandonment to Divine Providence which alone brings peace and joy to the soul.

Admittedly, one can never be completely free of the miseries inflicted by sickness, villainy or injustice, but we can choose to live gladly in the spirit of it all. Through faith we are capable of accepting the Master's grand design including the dark things that happen to us. On good days and bad, it is possible to reflect on the fact that God has an eternity of happiness waiting for us.

Wouldn't it be wonderful if on the deepest level of your being, you decided to be happy right now? On the surface you may have good reason to be sad, or you may be suffering in ways you cannot understand. Nevertheless, you are not a poor helpless creature. You have the power to lift up your heart and live gladly because of the knowledge of God's love. Why not try?

HOLY COMMUNION

By Fr. John T. Catoir, JCD | April 13, 2019

"`The Lord is kind and compassionate. He will not turn His face from you." (2 Chronicles 30:9)

"Knock and the door will be opened to you." (Matthew 7:7)

"The Lord is our refuge and our strength, a very present help in times of trouble." (Psalm 46:1)

oly Communion is the most precious gift that Jesus gave us. It is the perfect expression of God's unchanging love. The Eucharist is the real Presence of Christ on all the altars throughout the world.

In 2005, Cardinal Avery Dulles wrote, "This teaching surrounding the Eucharist remains as true and as normative today as it did from the beginning. The Council of Trent described the real Presence of Jesus with three adverbs: truly, really, and substantially."

Dulles continued, "The fathers and doctors of the Church have confidently proclaimed the real Presence century after century…the essential facts surrounding the mystery will always remain the same."

As with all other mysteries of faith, we stand in awe. We may not fully comprehend the mystery itself, but we are clear about the facts that surround the mystery. Take the mystery of Divine Love. The first fact about it is that it transcends human love. Humanly speaking, it is incomprehensible to us.

God is Love. God loves the sinner. We know this to be true because He died that sinners may be saved. However, since we cannot put our arms around God, difficulties arise. Jesus said, "Blessed are those who believe, even though they have not seen." One might express it this way: blessed are those who believe even if they do not fully comprehend the mystery itself.

However, difficulties do not amount to a single doubt. Doubters deny the truth and withhold their assent to all Divine mysteries. It's their loss. Believers accept the mysteries of revelation and they study the facts that surround each one.

For instance, we use the term 'transubstantiation' to describe how Christ's real Presence comes about in the Eucharist. The very substance of the bread and wine is changed into the hidden reality of the Risen Lord, Jesus Christ. Jesus becomes truly and substantially present at every Mass, under the appearances of bread and wine.

The Mass itself is a ritual which memorializes the one true sacrifice of Jesus Christ who gave up His life on Calvary in atonement for our sins. Jesus said, "Do this in memory of me," and we unite with Him, again and again, offering ourselves to the Father. God in turn says, "Fear not little one, for it is your Father's good pleasure to give you the kingdom." (Luke 12:32)

Catholics have been attending Masses from the early days of the formative Christian community. The crucifixion took place over two thousand years ago, and the faithful have celebrated Christ's redemptive act of suffering and death on the cross every day since, century after century, all over the world.

Jesus speaks to His beloved people and says,

"Come to me all you who are weary and burdened, and I will give you rest." (Matthew 11:28)

"For God so loved the world, that He gave His only begotten Son, that whosoever believes in Him should not perish, but have everlasting life." (John 3:16)

HOW TO MAKE A GOOD RETREAT
By Fr. John T. Catoir, JCD | July 26, 2018

In order to make a helpful retreat, you must plan ahead. Ask yourself what you hope to take away from the experience. Here's how I go about it. At the opening of every retreat I conduct I ask the retreatants, "What are you hoping to get from this weekend?"

Here is a sampling of the answers they give me: "I came to recharge my batteries; to be more comfortable with myself; to get better at talking to God; to be more hopeful and less negative; to hear God's voice telling me whether I'm still on the right track." The list goes on and on.

Then I explain the theme of the retreat I have prepared for them. I want our time together to be fruitful, so I challenge them right away. "God is calling you higher. He wants you to live more joyfully because of the knowledge of his love." This theme is taken from the words of Blessed Julian of Norwich, a 15th century English mystic who is revered for her joyful spirit. If you put this desire into practice, miracles will happen. Joy and self-respect will flow into your veins. The body and spirit are one. That means you are able to make your dreams come true.

Begin to practice living joyfully right away. It's a matter of skill development. You don't have to do anything to win God's love, but you do have to practice the virtues. Virtues turn into habits and good habits shape character. Think about it. Since fear and anger are the chief enemies of joy, you must strive to banish fear and anger from your psyche. Concentrate on joy. Lift up your heart more often and actually feel the joy of being alive. You are loved by God. That's a fantastic fact of life.

Now let's get specific. Suppose you want to get a better handle on your drinking. The founders of Alcoholics Anonymous (AA)—Bill Wilson and Bob Richards—recommend that you practice the "Third Step" of the "Twelve Step Program." This tells you to "turn your life and your will over to the God of your understanding." If you do that repeatedly, it will become a habit. AA makes the claim that if you truly turn everything over to Him, most especially your weakness, then God will do for you what you have not yet been able to do for yourself. He will take the craving for alcohol away. It's a fact. Millions of recovering addicts testify to this fact.

Some alcoholics think that sobriety is the goal of recovery. Not so! Living Joyfully is the goal. Liberation from guilt, anger, and negativity are the real goals. Some drinkers manage to stay away from booze, but they remain angry and bitter and continue to be miserable. I remind them of the beautiful words of Blessed Julian of Norwich, "The greatest honor you can give to Almighty God is to live joyfully because of the knowledge of God's love."

It is a goal worth pursuing, so make it your primary goal.

IMMATURITY AND MARRIAGE

By Fr. John T. Catoir, JCD | January 25, 1973

I t is always helpful to know what is going on in Rome. For those who are interested in keeping up with the evolving jurisprudence in the matrimonial tribunals of the world, I would like to present an excerpt taken from *Monitor Ecclesiasticus*, 1968-II, p. 306–314, of a case of nullity before the Appeal Tribunal of the Vicariate of Rome. The English translation of the decision rendered by Father Mark Said of the Pope's Appeal Tribunal is by Father James A. McEnerey, S.J. The following is an excerpt from the law section of the decision where an annulment was granted on the basis of immaturity. None of the facts of the specific case are mentioned.

"Canon 1081: Marriage is contracted by the legitimately manifested consent of two parties who are qualified by law to enter into such contracts: no substitute for consent can be supplied by any human power."

Msgr. Said's decision reads as follows: "Under this Canon (C.1081), as in a seed, can be included all defects because of which a marriage can be declared null because of defect of consent, as it is called, whether it is a question of amentia, OR lack of knowledge of the nature of marriage, OR defect of discretion and maturity of judgement, OR error concerning the person, OR simulation, OR a condition, and so on. In other words, Canon 1081 establishes and determines what a marriage ought to include from the law of nature and from the positive law in a general fashion with special emphasis on the human act necessary for marriage, and the object of that human act."

"Canon 1082: The matrimonial consent cannot be validly given unless the contracting parties know at least that marriage is a permanent union between man and woman for the procreation of children. Ignorance on this point is not presumed in persons who have attained the age of puberty."

The decision continues: "It is more than certain that if insufficient conceptual knowledge of the nature of marriage is possessed by a contracting party, i.e. he or she has no theoretical understanding of marriage as a permanent union involving sexual rights and obligations, the marriage must be declared null. It is also certain that speculative knowledge of the nature of marriage is not sufficient for the giving of a true matrimonial consent. Appreciative and estimative cognition, i.e. discretion and maturity of judgement on the part of the intellect is required in order that a deliberate matrimonial consent if given.

"Similarly, if the contracting party at the time of the celebration of the marriage were not capable, in a proportionate way of deliberation about the act being placed, i.e. did not have sufficient discretion and maturity of judgement which we call estimative knowledge of the nature of marriage, then the validity of the marriage will not be sustained, even if the contracting party did have conceptual knowledge of marriage. The reason is that this does not suffice for a true marriage consent as we have seen."

For the record, I want you to know that in the Diocese of Rome, in the Vicariate Appeal Tribunal, annulments have been granted on the basis of immaturity. If the Pope's marriage court has allowed this development in jurisprudence as far back and even before 1968, the faithful in the United States should not be scandalized if the same principles are applied in their own local tribunal.

There is a difficulty in establishing the degree of immaturity and for this, in most cases, we must ask the parties to undergo psychological testing at their own expense to obtain a more scientific assessment of the facts, but it is interesting to know that this avenue is no longer closed in our Church courts.

INNER PEACE DEPENDS ON YOU

By Fr. John T. Catoir, JCD | August 23, 2017

People have asked me: how do you prepare your soul to receive inner peace? It's a good question because inner peace is a gift from God, and you need to know how to accept it and make it your own.

A few obvious things might prevent you from gaining inner peace and they must be eliminated. Drug and alcohol abuse will cause needless cravings that disturb your peace. Anger and vindictiveness will stir your passions and create needless anxiety. Work on forgiveness.

But if you really want to go into training and are willing to overcome these obstacles, I have just what you need. It's a special prayer that will reap a harvest of blessings in your life.

The type of prayer I'm referring to is not based on your emotions; no need to beg or force feelings of any kind. True prayer is in the will. The will says yes or no. Cardinal Mercier, a 19th Century prelate from Belgium, wrote this prayer which captures the idea that true prayer is in the will to give yourself to God.

"Holy Spirit, Soul of My Soul, I adore you. Guide me, strengthen me, and console me. Tell me what to do. Give me your orders. I promise to submit to whatever you desire of me and accept everything you allow to happen to me. Let me only know your will."

Once you get into the habit of saying this prayer on a regular basis, your life will take on a new level of enthusiasm. Peace will come to you. Peace is the gateway of joy and spiritual joy is the infallible sign of the Holy Spirit.

I grant you, this prayer is a bit risky. What if God asked you to do something you don't want to do or something beyond your strength? Wouldn't that make you more anxious than ever? Yes, it might, but here's the rub. If you trust God, there's no need to doubt His love. He will always do right by you.

Remember, God designed you for a purpose. He knows what your heart wants and needs. He would never ask you to go against your conscience. Besides, He will supply all the strength you need for any challenge that life may present.

How do I know this? Because I've lived it for decades. If the truth be known, I didn't want to be a priest at first. I stubbornly resisted my vocation for years, but the secret desire for it was there all the time. I was just afraid. I'm so glad I took the risk.

Men and women from all walks of life have gone through this same type of struggle and felt God's strength guiding them through the storms of life. They turned their lives over to God and never looked back.

Once you attain a prayerful state of peace, your life will take on a meaning that this world cannot give. Wouldn't you like to speak and act spontaneously and not from fear? Wouldn't you like to enjoy the feeling that your soul is in harmony with God's will?

Say this prayer and no matter what your vocation is, you'll be on your way to true holiness.

JESUS AND THE BIBLE
By Fr. John T. Catoir, JCD | June 22, 2018

Of the approximately 107 billion human beings that have lived and died on planet Earth, Jesus Christ was by far the most outstanding, the most influential, and the most revered. He only lived 33 years among us. "He never wrote a book, he never held an office, he never went to college, and he never travelled more than 200 miles from where He was born. He did more things associated with greatness but had no credentials other than Himself." – Excerpt from *A Solitary Life* by Dr. James Allan, 1926

The Bible is a collection of 66 books written over a period of 1,500 years by dozens of authors in three different languages. They wrote during different periods of world history and couldn't possibly have collaborated with one another. Nevertheless, they produced a single book with one theme: the coming of the Messiah and the redemption He would provide.

There are 3,956 verses in the Bible, which are directly or indirectly concerned with prophesy about the coming of Jesus. Here is one from Zachariah 9:9: "Daughters of Zion, shout for joy, rejoice O daughters of Jerusalem, behold your king comes to you riding on a donkey." Hundreds of years before Jesus was born, hundreds of prophesies appeared revealing the circumstances of His birth. From the Book of Micah 5:2: "But you Bethlehem, though you be small among the clans of Jonah, out of you will come the ruler who will shepherd my people." Jesus fulfilled all the prophesies written about Him, including those describing His passion and death.

He's had more hospitals, orphanages, rescue missions and the like dedicated to Him than anyone. More human compassion and service efforts have been founded and financed by His followers than all other religions combined. Jesus is unparalleled as a "moral" influence. His life and teachings remain unsurpassed in their abilities to guide people and whole cultures toward altruism. He leads people out of confusion, doubt and misery. His artistic influence is utterly amazing. Jesus has inspired more of the world's great art, literature, and music than any person who has ever lived.

In America alone, 128 colleges have been dedicated to His teachings and values. Not only the Catholic Colleges, but also Harvard, Princeton, Yale and a host of others which were founded to prepare Christian ministers and missionaries.

No one has done more to secure the rights of women than Jesus. When He came into the world, women were still being traded for cattle. Few enjoyed marital rights and could be easily dismissed at the will of their marital masters. Because of Him, women have been ennobled and respected as never before.

The Lord's teaching on the dignity of the individual became the cornerstone of America's Declaration of Independence. The powerful influence of Jesus Christ on the history of the world cannot be underestimated, much less explained on the merely human level. Jesus Christ is not just a great man among many, He is God incarnate, the only begotten Son of Our Heavenly Father.

"This is my beloved Son in whom I am well pleased."(Matthew 3:17)

"All Scripture is inspired by God, and is profitable for teaching, for correcting, for training in righteousness, so that the people of God may be adequately equipped for every good work."(2 Timothy 3:16-17)

Follow Him and may the Lord be your strength and your joy.

P.S. I dedicate this article to the late Robert Newton Hunter, who inspired it by his great love of Jesus.

JESUS CHOSE A MARRIED PRIESTHOOD
By Fr. John T. Catoir, JCD | September 5, 2019

Sex abuse must be rooted out and the time has come for the Church to reexamine some of its policies. Jesus Christ required His priests to be men of faith; celibacy was not a priority. The clerical system we now have in place was instituted in 1139 A.D., at the Second Lateran Council. The bishops decided to split the Church into two categories: the clergy and the laity. Henceforth, the priesthood would consist of single men who were duty-bound to renounce marriage. This meant that a commitment to celibacy became a requirement for all future priests. The Council of Trent ratified this decision in 1563. It was understandable, single men were easier to control than families. Wives and children complicate things.

But by trying to solve one problem, did we create a bigger one? I think so. The sex abuse problem must be rooted out. Child abusers must be prevented from hiding secretly in the shadows. This horrific scandal has been going on too long and must be stopped.

Members of the hierarchy have been urging Pope Francis to create a blue-ribbon committee of the laity to help the hierarchy in searching for a solution. For too long, the laity has been kept out of the decision-making sessions where Church policy is decided. We need to enforce a no-tolerance policy. This means: one strike and you're out.

We need to return to the broader plan instituted by Jesus Christ and eliminate the celibacy requirement. Here's why!

1. We can simplify the vocation problem. Many men feel called to the priesthood but are discouraged by the celibacy restriction.
2. The role of women would be increased. Their wisdom would be much more available in the life of the Church, and they would be more respected.
3. Church unity would be given a boost. Many believe that the Protestant reformation was precipitated by the creation of clericalism with all its pomp and circumstance.
4. The humility of Jesus would be emphasized in Church life and titles like "Your Excellency" and "Your Eminence" would become passé.

It will take time to get all the wrinkles out, but many people are beginning to agree: drastic problems require drastic solutions. It can be done!

Celibacy attracted many holy men, but in the mix, there were a small number who were not so holy, a small minority who had other things on their minds. We must do a better job, a flawless job, of eliminating them.

Jesus knew what he was doing. There's an old saying: "A man is as good as the woman in his life." It may not be universally true, but there is enough truth in it for us to reexamine the necessity of celibacy in the life of the Church.

At 87, I'm not pushing to marry off our present crop of celibate priests, and I do understand that all this change might seem to be going too far for some tastes, but I think it doesn't go far enough. It would solve the vocation problem immediately and help us to begin the process of weeding out pedophiles. This will all take time, of course, but we would be returning to the system Jesus instituted, and that seems like a promising idea to me.

May the Lord be your strength and your joy as we weather this storm together.

JESUS SUFFERED FOR OUR SINS

By Fr. John T. Catoir, JCD | March 19, 2019

There are two kinds of sin: sins of weakness and sins of malice. Be very careful not to imitate the fallen angels who committed sins of malice. They claimed the right to offend Almighty God, similar to those who claim the right to murder their own child.

Jesus taught us the Golden Rule: "Do unto others as you would have them do unto you." Thank God your mother obeyed the law. Jesus always told the complete truth, "Do not do to others what you would not want them to do to you."

Jesus said, "I have come to bring joy." Pope John Paul II added, "Christ came to bring joy...joy to friends and families, joy to the sick and elderly; indeed, He came to bring joy to all people. Go, therefore, and become messengers of divine joy."

But doesn't the Cross dominate Christianity? How do we reconcile joy with the cross of Christ? For many, joy is very elusive. However, for many others joy is easily attainable. Millions of people are able to find joy in the sadness of their disability.

Robert Mueller was the former Executive Assistant to five Secretary Generals of the United Nations. He made this brilliant statement, "A vagabond in a ditch or an invalid in a bed can be a thousand times more joyful than an insatiable neurotic millionaire in his skyscraper."

I was privileged to be a friend of Robert Mueller for many years. We did two nationally syndicated TV shows together, as well as many radio shows. He was a gifted man, admired at the UN, and an inspiration to many world leaders. His words were always based on the wisdom of Jesus Christ.

Witnesses abound among both saints and sinners who have attained Joy, overcoming many forms of suffering and sorrow. Joy consists of an inner gladness that comes from the knowledge of God's love. If you choose to live in the Joy of Jesus, make His Joy a part of your life, and it will abide with you in all circumstances.

Here is more of Mueller's thinking:

"Decide to be cheerful. Render others cheerful. Praise the entire world with your cheer. Be a rock against sadness. Be optimistic and hopeful. Turn on your cheerful buttons and be grateful always."

There is a level of spirituality above our ordinary day-to-day existence which is rooted in the Joy of Jesus. Jesus said, "Faith can move mountains." Either you believe Him or not. But why not? Who wants to languish in misery? We do well when obey the Gospel! Faith is the acceptance of the mysteries of Divine Revelations. God's ways are not man's.

Doubt is hesitation over believing revealed truth. It leads to faithlessness. Outright disbelief is a sad option. On the other hand, there is great wisdom in accepting the truth of supernatural mysteries about God's Unchanging Love. There are many things in nature that are beyond our understanding, so too, in the supernatural order. Take for example the basic truth that Almighty God is all-powerful.

Once you believe that simple truth, the rest is easy. It is then no longer difficult to believe in God who became a man and grew in wisdom, age and grace; a God who loved the world so much that He suffered and died that we might live.

May the Lord be your strength and your JOY.

JOY PREVAILS OVER SORROW
By Fr. John T. Catoir, JCD | December 8, 2017

To master the art of living, it's important to understand this basic principle: Joy Prevails Over Sorrow. We know from divine revelation that there is an afterlife; where all our tears will be wiped away, and all the broken fences will be mended. The gift of eternal life is reason enough for rejoicing in the present moment.

A supernatural perspective is so important for attaining human happiness. Given all the miseries that befall every human life, I often wonder how the atheists manage to live joyfully, given their refusal to believe in the necessity of a first cause.

In my year-long correspondence with astronomer Carl Sagan, may he rest in peace, I asked him, "How can you conclude there is no God when everyone knows that something doesn't come from nothing? The cosmos, with all its precisely designed solar systems, must have had a Supreme Intelligence behind it."

He replied, "Why does there have to be a first cause. Maybe everything in the universe always was?" I said, "That's a big maybe. I wouldn't want to bet my life on a maybe". It seems to me that atheism is more a matter of the will than the intellect. The will to disbelieve in God's existence is often related to the desire to be free from any accountability to a Divine being.

Sooner or later, those who believe that the theory of evolution explains the origin of mankind must face the fact that it does not. Where did the oceans come from for the fish to evolve into humans?

I'd rather be a saint than a non-believer. Saints are grateful in all circumstances; they tend to rejoice both when it rains and when the sun shines. Saints are instinctively joyful because they believe deeply that God loves them. Their very joy is a sign of God's presence in them.

The greatest sorrow is not to be a saint. Good people who consider themselves saints-in-training, know down deep that everything that they've ever accomplished in life has only been possible through the grace and generosity of God. Once you accept the fact that God loves you, your life takes on a new meaning.

You then begin the process of 'Divinization'; i.e., the process of living joyfully, with a grateful heart in all circumstances. Divine revelation teaches us that God not only loves us, but that He wants us to love Him in return.

"The greatest honor we can give Almighty God is to live joyfully because of our belief in His love."– Blessed Julian of Norwich. From the time you were in your mother's womb, God loved you. He will continue to love you throughout your entire life.

If you are sorrowing over the loss of a loved one, or are experiencing a health problem, or suffering any heartache, please be brave. Believe with all your heart that God's love will bring you through all the storms of life until you are safely home with Him in heaven.

May the Lord be your strength and your joy.

LETTING LOVE IN DURING LENT

By Fr. John T. Catoir, JCD | February 24, 2018

My love goes out to all of you this holy season of Lent. Now that I am an old man, I see more clearly that love is the only thing that really matters in life. Things you have acquired, like wealth or power or fame, are not really important. All that matters is how much of God's love you've shared with those in need.

Every Lent we celebrate God's gifts, especially the gift of eternal life. We aspire to attain heaven by striving for greater perfection. As we approach the joy of Easter, we are facing the challenge of using our gifts well.

In his loving wisdom, God has given each of us two great gifts: a life to live and a love to share. St. Paul wrote: "But the greatest of these is love." (1 Corinthians 13:13). To have a good Lent, we all need to focus on the desires of the heart. Do you have the right attitude toward others?

Think about your gifts and talents. How are you using them? Focus on the ways your gifts can bring a smile to a child's face or a warm feeling to an elderly person in need of kindness.

Your talent for helping others should not become mere good intentions. Take action as best as you can. What are you good at? We all have talents that aren't used as well as they should. If there is something you enjoy doing, do it soon for someone who needs your special touch.

There is still time to think of ways to share your talents with the people you love. Bake a cake, sing a song or just be there for someone who needs a little cheer.

Since God delights in loving us, we need to take delight in loving others. We do this best by sharing our gifts with them. Spread your love around. You can break out and bring joy to those who have no claim on your kindness.

God's joy is contagious. Since you know that you are a carrier of divine love, why not figure out ways to help those near you? Think of ways to bring joy especially to those who may live in fear.

Fear is the enemy of joy. The reason God said to us in Isaiah 41:10, "Do not fear: I am with you. Do not be anxious; I am your

God. I will strengthen you, I will help you." He wants us to enjoy our lives. To begin doing that, we have to rid ourselves of needless worry. Immediately put on the will to bear discomfort and smile.

Some are better than others at shedding fear. I know this because I was born a worrier. I was born in 1931. My mother carried me in her womb for nine months during the Great Depression and my father was out of work. Her fears seeped into my genes.

Today I am free of all that because I made a concerted effort to trust God more and more. I no longer let anxiety get a foothold in my psyche. If fear does strike, I immediately think of it as a gift and a test to see how quickly I can show the Lord that I trust Him implicitly. His loving protection covers us in all circumstances.

MAJOR AND MINOR ADDICTIONS
By Fr. John T. Catoir, JCD | January 14, 2019

A few years ago, I wrote a column on the topic of "Cell Phone Addiction." Today I'm expanding my focus to include addictions of every kind. It's a well-known fact that minor addictions can disrupt your life, but major addictions can destroy your life.

People are glued to their iPods, cell phones, iPads, and computers. They text message all day long and in the process lose their ability to engage in the art of conversation while never developing the art of writing. Fewer and fewer people, young and old, write letters any more. This is sad but not fatal.

Parents are out of their wits trying to get their children's attention. If you investigate the problem of cell phone addiction, you'll be amazed to learn that many nations are way ahead of the U.S. in dealing with it. For instance, South Korea is the most wired country in the world. They have internet-counseling centers where youngsters are taught to combat computer compulsion by keeping themselves engaged with exercises and group activities. Many other countries have done the same thing. Kids need all the help they can get.

Over 50,000 people, young and old, in America are dying of drug-related causes every year. Minor addictions like marijuana (or 'pot') can create a predisposition to more serious addictions. Pot is known to be an entry level drug leading to the use of deadly illegal drugs. There's no magic bullet that can make addictions go away, especially when they become major addictions. The Opioid Epidemic alone takes many thousands of lives every year. Add to that, deaths from heroin, cocaine, ecstasy, and methamphetamine. Taken all together, you have more deaths in one year from drug use than the total death toll of the entire Vietnamese War which lasted about eight years.

Rather than dwell on these sad statistics, I'd prefer to close with a positive story from Anthony de Mello's book, *The Song of the Bird*. I've paraphrased it slightly. A young boy addicted to drugs opens the story with these words: "Everyone kept after me to change, and I resented it. And yet I agreed with them in a way I wanted to be free of the constant pressure to clean up my act, but I simply couldn't kick the habit. No matter how hard I tried I felt powerless and trapped. Then one day out of the blue, my father, who had grown weary of nagging me, said, 'Son – I give up. Don't change. I love you just as you are. Deal with this as best you can. I'm turning it all over to the Lord.' I suddenly felt free and less guilty. I still wanted to be free of drugs, but now I began to realize that I was the only one who could make it happen. When I realized that my father would continue to love me whether I changed or not, something happened inside of me. And, believe it or not, I went on to become drug-free."

Everyone is unique. Some remedies may work for one person and not another, but it's always wise to bring the Lord into the picture – and the sooner the better. Trying to help someone free themselves from an addiction is not something you should try on your own. Get help, both from neighbors and from God. It's always good to know that you can put your trust in the Lord and get results. Believe deeply and do not fear, for Jesus said, "Fear is useless, what you need is trust."

MEDITATION AND LONELINESS

By Fr. John T. Catoir, JCD | October 15, 2018

Billions of men and women down through the ages have tried to solve the problem of loneliness, each in his or her own way. Even the saints suffer from loneliness. St. Augustine described it as the human condition, "Our hearts are restless until they rest in Thee O Lord."

Begin by accepting the fact that loneliness is basic to human nature. Even husbands and wives experience it because metaphysical loneliness is the price we pay for being unique. We are utterly different. That is a universal fact of life, and a spiritual problem. You experience loneliness because your soul longs for the living God.

Consider this: if you put the pain of loneliness next to all the problems you've had to cope with in 2018, like the political unrest over Judge Kavanaugh's nomination, the starkness of your isolation has never been more evident and upsetting. Political opinions put us at odds with one another. In some families, members argue fiercely with loved ones thus separating them further apart from one another.

Going forward, what's the answer? I don't have a simple answer, but I think there's one remedy we can all agree on; namely, that attitude is important. Your attitude can make an enormous difference. With the right attitude life can move along much more peacefully and more joyfully.

Meditation is one of the best ways to achieve the proper attitude. It helps you to calm yourself down, increase your joys, and minimize your sorrows. Achieving control over your emotions is easier said than done, but psychiatrists agree that happiness is a choice and meditation is one of the best resources we have in controlling our outlook.

Turn off the cell phone, the TV, and all the electronic devices that compete for your attention. On a regular basis, remove yourself from the fray and take inventory. Relax in silence. Put on the will to listen to yourself breathing. Thank the Lord for all your blessings. Really pause and be grateful.

By reminding yourself of the importance of meditation, I hope you will be able to put on a protective shield that will save you from your worst faults and failings. It's free of charge and available at all hours of the day and night. Many lives have been ruined by anger and the loss of self-control. People are murdered and severely hurt, relationships are broken, and all kinds of misery ensues. Words and actions can do a lot of harm. The loss of common sense in a fit of anger can be devastating.

Regaining one's self-control becomes possible with the frequent practice of meditation. Learn how to master yourself and you'll avoid much needless suffering. Invite God into the situation. Jesus said, "Seek first the Kingdom of God." Surround yourself with silence and count to ten. Focus on your own breathing. Sit quietly for a time, and day-dream about peace of soul. Abide in the Lord. By doing this you will be more appreciative of your friends and loved ones. Don't be negative. With God's help, you can do all things.

Learn how to be your own best friend, and not your own worst enemy. Love God and become more holy. This would please the Lord immensely. God bless you and may the Lord be your strength and your joy as you work your way through the storms of life.

MODERN SKEPTICISM AND YOU

By Fr. John T. Catoir, JCD | August 20, 2017

Skepticism has always been with us. Jesus dealt with it frequently, "O you of little faith," (Matthew 6:30). Today we are living in the age of science and skepticism is widespread. Apart from the influence of science itself, we can trace the philosophical roots of skepticism back to the 17th Century.

Rene Descartes (1596-1650), who is the Father of Modern Philosophy, challenged the way we know things. He rejected everything that is derived from faith alone, and went on a search to justify anything he believed on the basis of reason alone.

His first question was, "How do I even know that I exist?" Most sane people take their own existence for granted. Descartes was sane, but he needed to be able to prove his existence, scientifically.

His "eureka moment" came when it suddenly occurred to him that since he was a thinking person, he must exist. Thus, the famous line, "I think therefore I am", in Latin, *cogito ergo sum.*

A century later, Immanuel Kant (1724-1804), the famous German skeptic, applied this approach to the interpretation of Sacred Scripture. Until then, the reading of scripture was pretty much a straightforward exercise. You study the text and assume that it says exactly what the sacred author intended.

But, of course, we soon learn that we cannot take every word in scripture literally. Jesus called Herod a fox; does that mean he had four legs and a tail? Of course not. It's merely a figure of speech meaning that Herod was crafty and shrewd. We know there are metaphors in scripture and other forms of hidden meanings that need authoritative interpretation.

Catholics have always accepted the guidance of the Church in the interpretation of scriptural passages. We simply consult the Church's teaching authority, and ask, 'what did the sacred author mean when he wrote this particular passage?' We try to stay out of error by following the truths found in the Church's Deposit of Faith, as expressed in the Nicene Creed.

According to Kant and his followers, however, our creed is a mere folk tale, and the divinity of Christ is a myth. These are the heresies that have spawned a steady wave of confusion among believers and non-believers alike in this modern age.

Once the authority of the Church is dismissed, the interpretation of scripture is left to the individual. Self-appointed Biblical scholars then come on the scene and begin disagreeing with one another on essential points of doctrine.

Private interpretation has become so widespread and varied that one group of theologians decided to follow the principle of "Majority Rule." Sixty of them may hold for one opinion, while thirteen may hold another. Evangelical Christians rejected this approach and decided to interpret everything literally.

From the beginning, Roman Catholics have always believed that when Jesus said, "This is my body", he meant it literally. The Eucharist is the Real Presence of Jesus under the appearance of bread and wine. Dissenters say, "the bread remains mere bread."

We need the objective authority of the Church to keep us on track. The Divine element of the Church sustains us throughout our lives; the human element often falls into error and needs correction. Either you understand this and agree with it or not.

Jesus calls you to be a person of great faith. "Blessed are those who have not seen and yet believe." (John 20:29)

MOTHER THERESA AND C.S. LEWIS

By Fr. John T. Catoir, JCD | July 18, 2018

The thing I remember most about St. Mother Theresa was her joy. I met her three times in my life. Once when we were giving talks on the same program, once at a Vatican Seminar on Family Life, and once when she asked me to give a week-long retreat on Joy to her contemplative novices. She founded two distinct orders; the one she picked for me was her Cloistered Contemplative community in Northern New Jersey.

I was intimidated, of course. After all, this was THE Mother Theresa and a week is a long time to keep talking, but she gave me courage. I remember a quote of hers: "Joy is prayer. Joy is strength. Joy is love. Joy is a net of love by which you can catch souls. You give the most when you give joy. God loves a cheerful giver. Never let anything so fill you with sorrow as to make you forget the joy of Christ risen."

The retreat went very well and the Sisters took their solemn vows and eventually went on to serve all over the world. Mother always had her contemplatives go out of the convent each day to ask people if they wanted the sisters to pray for anyone in the family. It was a much-appreciated innovation to tradition of cloistered living. I admired her as much as I did C.S. Lewis.

Lewis was a Christian writer who had no peer when it came to challenging skeptics and atheists. It may come as a surprise to learn that Clive Staples Lewis was himself an atheist most of his adult life. I never met him, but I admired him greatly. His mysterious conversion from non-belief to such an exemplary level of faith was surely a miracle. I hope it gives hope to many Catholic parents who have seen their sons and daughters fall away from the Church. Lewis taught that our goal is to proclaim the reality of the Kingdom of God's love and joy. The secular culture has lost its sense of God, its sense of sin, and its sense of the sacredness of life. Evangelization, Lewis insisted, is more a matter of prayer and personal holiness than of making proclamations from a soapbox.

In his book, *Mere Christianity*, Lewis wrote, "If you read history, you will find that the Christians who did the most for the present world were those who thought most about the next." The Lord's Prayer contains the words: "deliver us from evil." Lewis believed that we should pray with conviction to be delivered from evil powers. He said, "the power of choice makes evil possible, but choice is also the only thing that makes possible any love, goodness or joy worth having."

He urged us to choose love and joy. Pray that your loved ones will be delivered from evil, so they may come to the knowledge of God's love and joy. It is the vision of the Holy that has produced many of the masterpieces of art and music. This same vision motivates the faithful to risk everything to relieve the world's suffering: caring for plague victims, defending the rights of children, guiding slaves to freedom, breaching war zones to feed the poor."

MY EARLY DAYS AS A PRIEST

By Fr. John T. Catoir, JCD | October 3, 2018

After serving as a priest for 58 years, I'm often asked by people who knew that I was a native New Yorker, how I became a priest of the Diocese of Paterson, New Jersey. I was born in Manhattan, raised in St. Joan of Arc Parish, Jackson Heights, Queens, and I graduated from Fordham University in 1953. The Korean War was still winding down when I was drafted into the U.S. Army. I served my first year as a Military Policeman and my second year as a Chaplain's assistant.

I knew that I wanted to be a priest, so after my discharge I immediately made an appointment with the Brooklyn Diocesan Chancellor, who told me that their Seminary was at full capacity, and that I lacked any College credits in Greek. I was very disappointed. Not knowing what to do next, I went to the Dean of Fordham University and asked him to help me get enough credits in Greek to make myself more acceptable. He told me that even if I took some courses, I'd have no guarantee that they would accept me because of the volume of candidates.

I still vividly remember his next few words, "Across the Hudson River in New Jersey, the Paterson Diocese is desperately in need of vocations, why not apply there?" I decided instead to apply to the New York Archdiocese. They told me the same thing, "no room at the inn." I finally realized that this was Divine Providence at work and reconciled myself to the will of God. I applied for admission to Paterson and was immediately accepted. After my ordination in 1960, they sent me off to Catholic University in Washington, D.C. to get a doctorate in Canon Law.

When I returned with my JCD three years later, they made me the assistant pastor at St. Brendan's parish in Clifton, New Jersey, and I was happy at last. As an afterthought, I was also told that I would oversee the diocesan Marriage Tribunal part-time. It was hard at first, but I gradually began to see it all as a blessing in disguise. I had been given the power to help many Divorced people who were suffering severely, and I began to understand how the rigid application of canon law was denying them true justice. So, gradually, I began encouraging some of them to return to the sacraments based on their good conscience.

For your information, that's another reason why I'm a huge fan of Pope Francis. He has encouraged Catholics in certain circumstances to rely more on conscience than on the letter of the law, which always presumes that people are living in a state of mortal sin. The fact that we have annulments testifies to the fact that often these early presumptions turn out to be false. God knows that perfection in all circumstances is beyond heroic virtue and He only calls on us to make a reasonable effort to be good. Perfection is humanly impossible. The enemies of the Pope are quick to condemn people, including the Pope himself, and slow to "lift a finger to help them" as Jesus put it so wisely centuries ago.

The Holy Spirit often leads us in directions that favor mercy over legalism. God bless you for your patience in these challenging times.

MY FATHER

By Fr. John T. Catoir, JCD | June 2, 2018

The two greatest gifts my father gave me were his love for my mother, and his faith in Jesus Christ. His love gave me the essential emotional security I needed growing up. It provided an atmosphere of emotional comfort and peace.

His faith gave me a solid foundation of knowledge concerning the supernatural world. From this I found my purpose and direction. I was never a pious kid. My vocation didn't dawn on me early, but I accepted the idea of heaven, and knew that I wanted to end up there.

I remember my first Holy Communion as a joyful occasion. No doubt it set the stage for my life-long vocation. But as soon as I became

a teen, I didn't want to be a priest; I wanted marriage and a family. It took time to arrive at self-understanding.

My Dad's father died when he was two. He was raised by a single mother who came from Ireland. She raised him working as a chambermaid in the Commodore Hotel. He attended St. Steven's Catholic School on 29th Street in New York where, coincidently, I lived in residence many years later while I was Director of The Christophers. I remember looking down from my rectory window on the school yard where my father played as a child.

Dad only had two years of high school before he went to work as a brick layer. He met my mother at a parish dance and they married two years later. New York was prosperous in those days and he was earning good money. Then came the market crash in 1929. He lost his job and was still out of work when I was born in 1931.

He managed to get an entry level job at Metropolitan Life and soon became a book keeper. He was the head of the Authenticating Department when he retired.

We had fun. I remember when I was about three, he had me step on his right hand, and then he'd raise me up over his head and parade me about the beach. I felt ten feet tall. He taught me how to fall on his other arm, promising me he'd never drop me. And he never did. I think that experience taught me to trust God the Father as I was growing up.

In those early years, after my sister Cathy was born, he got a second job as a house detective at the Roosevelt Hotel. He worked incognito at evening parties and was always ready to take out unruly guests if trouble arose. He worked these two jobs for many years to make a comfortable home for us.

We had many father-son talks as I was growing up. Thinking back and realizing that he never knew what it was to have a father of his own, he must have learned his fathering skills by instinct. Even so, he did a splendid job.

My wonderful mother died in 1957 and Dad was severely grief-stricken. By that time, I was in the seminary having already served two years in the Army. I'm nearly 87 as I write this article, and I still miss both my parents.

How blessed I am to have shared in the love of a great father and mother. Thanks be to God.

MY FAVORITE MOVIES
By Fr. John T. Catoir, JCD | January 15, 2018

Sweeping biographies about great leaders like Lincoln, Gandhi and Churchill are at the top of my list of favorite movies. I also love musicals. Up until recently, my favorite musical was *My Fair Lady*. However, *The Greatest Showman* has recently moved into first place.

From the opening scene, this movie about B.T. Barnum, was a joyful celebration. Hugh Jackman, and a great cast, lit up the screen with a series of unique musical sequences. However, when I praised the movie on Twitter, a woman took me to task.

She protested, "Barnum and his circus exploited human beings as freaks, and abused animals". I was shocked. The thought had never occurred to me. Why was I so insensitive? Then I realized that you can't really abuse animals, and expect them to stay under your control. I had doubts about that part of her assertion.

In the movie, the animals were shown a lot of love. On the other assertion that humans were exploited, I was perplexed. Maybe I was lulled by the fact that all the circus performers, the so-called "freaks", considered Barnum to be a father figure.

They had been outcasts their entire lives, rejected by the world until he gave them a job and a community of people who accepted them. They never had this before. They loved him and called themselves a family.

Or, maybe I enjoyed it so much because of its message, which was about repentance and redemption. Hugh Jackman's character, Barnum, after a tragic episode, blamed himself and made this profound statement, "It all happened because I thought I was more than I am." The movie was a dazzling morality play, which had a profound message: "Pride goes before the fall."

After I absolved myself, I moved on to a more philosophical question, "How should anyone judge a movie? Should we judge it based on the moral character of the leading man or woman?" No! Scoundrels need to be punished.

I loved *My Fair Lady* even though Professor Henry Higgins was an obnoxious snob who thoroughly abused Eliza Doolittle. I loved it because Audrey gets to put Rex in his place, and because it had a happy ending. George Bernard Shaw, the author of the play *Pygmalion*, on which *My Fair Lady* was based, took the story from Greek mythology.

Pygmalion was an artist who fell in love with one of his marble sculptures. Miraculously, she comes to life and begins to torment him. Alas, even the ancient Greeks had a sense of humor.

A play or a movie must be judged as a whole. The beginning, middle, and the end must all be taken into consideration. At that point you can make a determination: how did this experience make you feel?

My Fair Lady and *The Greatest Showman* made me feel good, full of joy and elation. It was well worth the price of admission.

With all that having been said, let's go back to the lesson which *The Greatest Showman* proclaimed: Strive to attain the virtue of humility, respect your neighbor as you would want them to respect you, be honest enough to admit your mistakes, and do all you can to make amends.

May the Lord be your strength and your joy.

MY INTERVIEW WITH MR. FRED ROGERS
By Fr. John T. Catoir, JCD

Fred Rogers was a good friend of mine for many years. He entertained and educated children for more than a generation. He died on February 23, 2003. Children love him and parents trust him. When he came to New York, we often had dinner together. I had the privilege of interviewing him on my TV show *Christopher Closeup*. The following is part of that interview:

FR. JOHN: The theme song of your TV Show *Mr. Roger's Neighborhood* contains the words, "Won't you be my neighbor?" Let me begin by asking, Why did you write those words, Mr. Rogers?

FRED ROGERS: When I hear words like those, I think the person speaking them cares about me. And I want them to know that I care about them and all children. I want them to feel that each one of them is special.

FR. JOHN: Your new book is entitled *"You are Special."* Tell us a little about it.

FRED ROGERS: I've collected lots of quotes and sayings over the last forty years, and they all describe how I feel about the person I am with at the moment. It is one of the most glorious things you can do in life, making the person you are with feel special. Evil in the world would want us to feel as awful as we could about who we are. But Jesus wants us to look at ourselves and our neighbor and see the best. How

wonderful it would be if we all became an advocate in life rather than an accuser.

FR. JOHN: In other words, promoting the person you're with, not tearing down.

FRED ROGERS: Exactly, that's a wonderful way of putting it.

FR. JOHN: You see your work on TV as a kind of ministry, don't you?

FRED ROGERS: Well yes. Years ago, when I had already started doing the children's TV show, people suggested that I should take some courses in theology and ministry, and I thought that might be interesting. So I began doing it on my lunch hour, and the process went on for eight years. Finally, they said that I actually had accumulated enough course credits to get ordained. So to my surprise, I was able to become an ordained minister. And the Church commissioned me to perform my ministry on TV, primarily working with families with young children.

FR. JOHN: How do you select the themes for your show?

FRED ROGERS: Many ideas come from the mail we receive. Who would have thought years ago that we would one day do a whole show on divorce? But children need to know that it is not their fault when their parents separate. Little children tend to think that the world revolves around them. And so consequently anything that happens to them must be because of them; as though the divorce was their fault. They think that it must be "something I did." If a child spills the milk at breakfast and it leads to loud talking between the parents, the child thinks he or she was at fault for causing the breakup. We try to get through to them that divorce is something that only has to do with adults, not children.

FR. JOHN: Fred, I know you try to get beneath the surface of things yourself. I wonder, can you tell me how your work affects the children you are reaching?

FRED ROGERS: A lot of people write to us. We get a sense that we are making a difference. I remember a letter I received recently. It was from an adult who had watched the show during his childhood, and he talked of the things he learned from Mr. Rogers growing up. It was very touching.

FR. JOHN: I heard a story that you were visiting Texas and signing autographs when a little boy came up to you. You asked his name and he replied, "Bobby," and you said, "Where do you live, Bobby?" And he answered quizzically, "You know!" presuming that you had to know, since you came into his home every day on TV.

FRED ROGERS: Yes, there have been many incidents like that. Sometimes they would ask, "How did you get out?" They must think I live in that TV set or somewhere in the neighborhood.

FR. JOHN: What has been your greatest satisfaction Fred?

FRED ROGERS: To be able to offer silence thru television. There isn't a lot of it out there.

FR. JOHN: How do you do that?

FRED ROGERS: Well, there are times when I don't say anything. I might be doing something, and they just watch me. I might be fixing something, or building something, but I don't speak. I did that in my book, *"You Are Special."* I think the spaces between the words on a page are sometimes more important than the words themselves. I have offered these great quotes, separated by a lot of white paper. It gives the reader space to breath in the meaning. For instance, a seminary professor of mine once said, "The only thing that evil cannot stand is forgiveness."

FR. JOHN: In other words, you are who you are; you do not present a false front to the world. Fred, what else do you think is important to do for the children?

FRED ROGERS: I think we have to provide them with heroes; like teachers who really believe that the only reason they are in the classroom is to help the children; or community leaders who see a gang as nothing more than a cluster of kids trying to make it through life. Heroes are important in life because we all need to look up to people. Many people we have on our show are unsung heroes. Those people who are not heroes like to say, "It's not my community! It's not my child!" They don't want to be involved. But heroes are the ones who step forward and take some responsibility for the happiness of others. They want to make this a better world.

FR. JOHN: So many people are saints and they don't even know it. You bring that to the TV screen every day. Fred, how would you answer this question? What do you wish for the parents who watch you?

FRED ROGERS: I would want them to listen to their own childhood which still resides within them, and allow that child to know that he or she is unique. Every time I walk into my TV studio I say a prayer, "Dear Lord, let some word that is heard today be Your word, because the rest is merely dross." And I would hope that both parents and children would allow that word to become part of who they are in this world.

FR. JOHN: Beautifully spoken. Thank you, Fred Rogers, for this delightful Christopher Closeup visit.

MY VOCATION

By Fr. John T. Catoir, JCD | June 20, 2018

My vocation is based on a lengthy conversation I had with God that began in 1945 during my senior year in high school. I came home from a retreat dreaming about being a priest. The idea had never really hit me so hard before, even though I had been an altar boy for three years in grammar school. The conversation I had with God was straightforward, and I kept telling Him, "I'll think about it".

I was thirteen at the time and began noticing the girls. Soon the idea of a vocation began fading from my consciousness. I became a normal teenager and never told a soul about my priesthood dreams. I had previously made a deal with God about getting into heaven and agreed to strive for holiness by staying in the state of grace. So, my roving eye was pretty much impeded from any serious action, even though I still had an eye for the girls. I wanted to marry one day and have a family. The desire to be a priest never went entirely away. All through college and the military service it would come back, at times with intensity.

In 1953, after graduation, as the Korean War was winding down, I was drafted and served stateside as a Military Policeman for a year, and a Chaplain's Assistant for my last year. I worried constantly, "What am I going to do when I get out?" It finally came

time to make a decision. I realized down deep that I wanted to be a priest more than anything, but I was afraid of failing and didn't want to risk it. God's grace relieved me of my fears, and I surrendered at last; "Yes Lord! I'll risk it! But you must promise to strengthen me and help me to bear rich and abundant good fruit. Alleluia!" He agreed, as I knew He would, and the deal was made in cement. This final surrender gave me the peace I needed to move forward, and I never looked back.

The rest is history. I had to delay entering the seminary a year because my mother was sick. I entered in 1956, and four years later I was ordained on May 28, 1960. It was the happiest day of my life. I served in the active ministry for forty years but had to retire because of prostate cancer surgery. I don't make any distinction between my active and retirement years because they were all part of the same deal I made with God. I offered my whole life.

Now, instead of parish work and being the Judicial Vicar of the Diocesan Marriage Tribunal, and later Director of The Christophers for 17 years with a nationally syndicated TV show, and finally running a soup kitchen and homeless shelter before retiring, I fiddle

(Photo: Dale Dexter)

with my syndicated column and my Tweets and posts on social media. So far, I have nearly 16,000 followers with 5,000 being regular followers who re-tweet my spiritual messages to millions of readers worldwide.

This sounds like bragging, I know, but I promised God that I'd make it clear to everyone that a girl-crazy teen could not have pulled this off on his own. God gets all the glory, and I thank Him with all my heart.

Everyone has a calling to become holy. May the Lord be your strength and your joy as you work through your vocation.

NATURE VS. NURTURE

By Fr. John T. Catoir, JCD | January 28, 2018

We all have character traits that are inherited. This is our nature. We also have characteristics that were developed over the years through training and societal influences. This is due to the way we were nurtured. Nurturing is meant to refine our nature.

Members of the same family have profoundly different personalities although they share the same gene pool. Countless generations have contributed to the mix, and God only knows the origin of some of the glaring negative traits that may befall any individual member of the family.

Every family has an old ancestor that had only one oar in the water. Pope Francis recently said, "There is no perfect family." The mix of national backgrounds makes every family utterly unique and sets apart each member from everyone.

In my opinion, parents are too hard on themselves when one of the children fails to live up to their hopes and dreams. There are two consequences that flow from this fact; 1. People needlessly blame themselves when things do not go as planned; and 2. Conflicts will always arise, and every family needs a problem solver to manage the peace.

1. The question should never be, "Who is to blame?" Sometimes nature takes over, and suddenly, all the good nurturing is overcome by an inherited impulse. And sometimes, outside influences can destroy all your good training and lead your loved one astray. This is not your fault! Better to pray more and blame less. Prayer is very important in achieving family unity. "Help us, O Lord, to be of one mind and heart in our care for one another."

2. There are an infinite variety of conflicts in every family. They often arise from our hidden assumptions. Whether it be in the family, the factory, or the monastery; if you find yourself in the middle of a conflict, it will help immensely if you strive to be a problem solver. Start by reflecting on some of your basic assumptions.

We are not all equal in our understanding of one another's needs. Sometimes we assume "my rights are superior to your rights". But each person's needs deserve to be acknowledged, even the youngest person in the conflict.

Some people are fighters for their rights and needs. Some are compromisers. Some are sore losers. Thank God some are problem solvers. They possess a skill that can be learned. Think about it.

By nature, a fighter is mistrustful and refuses to lose, demanding proof of the other person's needs. By nature, a compromiser is ready to give in, but in the end forfeits too much for the sake of peace. And by nature, sore losers walk away sulking holding on to grudges forever.

A problem solver rises above nature. A problem solver listens and tries to get to the root issue, while hoping to reach a compromise. The problem solver knows that a conflict does not mean that there must be a winner or a loser. The whole art of compromise rests on the fact that a win-win outcome is possible.

In summary, don't blame yourself for a loved one's failure to reach out for help, and don't allow petty conflicts to fester without reaching a compromise. Bring the parties together, admit that each side has certain rights, and work toward a win-win solution.

May the Lord be your strength and your joy.

NEWMAN AND YOUR NEW YEAR RESOLUTIONS
By Fr. John T. Catoir, JCD | 1970s

W hen you begin to think about New Year resolutions try to make Jesus Christ the centerpiece. To accomplish this, I'd like to share some thoughts with you taken from the greatest theologian of the nineteenth century, Cardinal John Henry Newman (February 21, 1801–August 11, 1890).

Newman was born in England and became an Episcopal priest in 1825. He led the Oxford

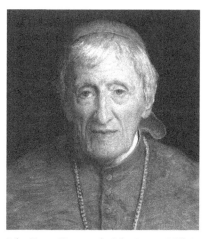

John Henry Newman by John Everett Millais

movement, which emphasized the Church Fathers as an important source of spiritual truth. His sermons were controversial because he preached in favor of Church tradition against the idea that scripture is the sole source of truth and wisdom. Luther proclaimed: "sola scriptura" at the beginning of the Reformation.

In 1841, Newman began doubting the claims of the Anglican Church, and eventually resigned his post at St. Mary's parish in the village of Littlemore, England. On October 9, 1845 he was received into the Roman Catholic Church. This was a courageous move which brought him a great deal of grief, but he attributed his strength through it all to Jesus whom he proclaimed as his Lord and Master.

One of Newman's main contributions was in the field of psychological analysis rather than in theology 'per se'. He saw doctrine as a living thing and compared it to the idea of human development. It's very important to understand him in the context of his devotion to the historical Jesus. Newman believed that the Incarnation, God becoming man, was the central truth of Christianity, and that Jesus constitutes the source of all spiritual power.

He died 125 years ago, and was beatified by Pope Benedict XVI in 2010. Another miracle is needed before he will be numbered among the canonized saints. Newman wrote the following prayer which is a beautiful expression of his total dependence of Jesus. Perhaps it will inspire you in making some New Year resolutions, as it did for me.

Teach me Lord to be sweet and gentle in the events of life,
in disappointments, in the thoughtlessness of others,
in the insincerity of those on whom I relied,
Let me put myself aside,
to think of the happiness of others,
to hide my little pains and heartaches,
so that I may be the only one to suffer from them.
Teach me to profit by the suffering that come across my path,
let me use it that it may mellow me, not harden and embitter me,
that it may make me patient, not irritable,
that it may make me broad in my forgiveness,
not narrow, haughty or overbearing.
May no one be less good for having come within my influence,
no one less pure, less true, less kind, less noble
for having been a fellow traveler in our journey toward eternal life.
As I go my rounds, from one distraction to another,
let me whisper, from time to time, a word of love to You.
May my life be lived in the supernatural,
full of power for good, and strong in its purpose of sanctity.

Dear Jesus, help me to spread your fragrance everywhere. Flood my soul with your spirit and life. Penetrate and possess my whole being so completely that my life may be only a radiance of Yours. Shine through me and be so in me that every soul I come in contact with may feel your presence in my soul. Let them look up and see me no longer, but only Jesus.

ON BEING A BETTER PASTOR

By Fr. John T. Catoir, JCD | August 1, 2019

I wish I had read the book, *The Better Pastor* by Patrick Lencioni, a layman who specializes in leadership and team building, earlier in my life. The book flap reads: "As he approached the door to the Sacristy, Fr. Daniel Connor had no idea that his parish and his priesthood – was about to be changed forever."

This book is a fictional, yet realistic story; lovingly written for all those priests in the world who are not only spiritual shepherds, but also leaders of the organizations we call parishes. Being the pastor of a Catholic parish is one of the most challenging jobs in the world. Whether they are responsible for a small rural parish, a medium-sized urban one, or a large suburban mega-parish — all pastors have one thing in common: they can't do it alone.

Though it's been a long time since I served as a pastor, I found this book to be extremely helpful, and an easy read. Unfortunately, many wonderful priests find that becoming a pastor can be overwhelming and lonely. It can diminish the joy of their vocation, which is a needless tragedy. That's the opinion of the author, and I agree with him. He has written best-selling books on leadership for businessmen and applied the same skills to parish life.

Here's an introduction in his own words:

1. A pastor is not just a priest but the leader of an organization that requires management and leadership skills.

2. Part of leading an organization is holding people accountable for excellence, which often involves difficult, uncomfortable, yet loving conversations.
3. A pastor needs a real management team to do this.
4. A pastor needs support from "outsiders" and other priests.

The Mass, which is the source and summit of our faith, is the most visible sign of the health of a parish. Excellence in the celebration of mass encourages parishioners and visitors to become more involved in going deeper in their faith and parish life. All of this will take time, involve pain, if an honest job report has to be issued. Don't back off and accept mediocrity.

Explore some amazing websites. Read great books on this topic. Pray and enlist others to ask God's help in achieving the goal of being the pastor God wants you to be.

May the Lord be your strength and your joy.

OUR FATHER

By Fr. John T. Catoir, JCD | 1970s

Words are semantic instruments created to give expression to living thoughts and ideas. When Christ instructed us about prayer, he told us not to babble like the heathens, uttering many words. Then he gave us a few profound words to say in the "Our Father."

To me, "Our Father" is a love song. God, our eternal Lover, has written a love song for His children.

OUR FATHER, WHO ART IN HEAVEN, HALLOWED BE THEY NAME...

"Our Father, in You the whole human race and all living things, find their source and sustenance. I bow before You with a heart full of joy and I pray that all other hearts will be inflamed with love at the very mention of Your name."

THY KINGDOM COME...

"Your Kingdom has already begun and I hunger for the day when Justice and peace will triumph and all Your children will know the fullness of joy which You have promised.

THY WILL BE DONE ON EARTH AS IT IS IN HEAVEN...

"Your will is my nourishment and life. I want to please You in every work and deed. I want to make Your love reign in this world, as it does in paradise, our true home."

GIVE US THIS DAY OUR DAILY BEAD...

"Father, we are weak, give us the strength to persevere in Your love, just for today; feed our deepest hunger and help us to love one another as You have loved us."

AND FORGIVE US OUR TRESPASSES AS WE FORGIVE THOSE WHO TRESPASS AGAINST US...

"Oh Lord, forgive me for failing to become a creature of love and joy: put into my heart the spirit of forgiveness and compassion for anyone who has failed me in any way. I am ever mindful of Your forgiveness of my sins and I thank You.

LEAD US NOT INTO TEMPTATION, BUT DELIVER US FROM EVIL...

"Heavenly Father protect us against our weaknesses and deliver us from the doubts and fears which undermine our confidence in Your loving presence. Free us from our selfish desires, which have so often betrayed us. We ask this in the Name of Jesus, whom You sent to lead us home.

All glory, power and praise be to You, Father, forever and ever, Amen.

OUR HEARTS ARE RESTLESS
By Fr. John T. Catoir, JCD | January 10, 2018

Many good people, men, women and children, are too critical of themselves. They often feel a strange restlessness that seems to have no explanation. If you're one of these people, let me try to put your mind at ease.

Saint Augustine once said, "Our hearts are restless until they rest in thee O Lord." This little quote can go a long way in helping you to understand the truth that restlessness is a part of the human condition. It's in our nature to experience a kind of separation anxiety in our relationship with God.

This may be difficult to understand, but there is a silent longing for God in the soul of every human being. God Himself put it there. So, there's nothing wrong with you except perhaps a little homesickness for heaven.

St. Frances de Sales offered this advice, "Don't be anxious because you're anxious." Spiritual solace will come to you once you accept the fact that this type of anxiety is normal. Self-understanding is necessary for self-acceptance, and you need self-acceptance in order to love yourself.

Of course, there are those who have no understanding of who they are, where they came from, or where they're going. These folks would deny the idea of a religious separation anxiety. They just blame the feeling on something else.

The more unfortunate ones are tempted to commit suicide. Please pray for them. It's a shame because there is an effective remedy available to help them – namely, contemplation. This type of prayer can soothe a troubled soul and alleviate loneliness. It goes beyond vocal or memorized prayer in the art of communicating with God.

Benedictine Abbot John Chapman explained it this way: "Pure prayer is not found in your words or feelings, you never have to force feelings of any kind. Pure prayer is in the will to give yourself to God."

Contemplation is wordless prayer. It need not be lengthy. The best way to pray is to pray often; i.e., give yourself to God frequently during the day. Your sense of intimacy with God will increase, and your separation anxiety will diminish.

This requires faith, of course, but you have faith and it doesn't have to be particularly strong. Remember the words of Jesus. "If you have faith the size of a mustard seed, you will be able to move mountains." (Matthew 17:20)

In other words, you have enough faith when you know that the Love of God extends to every human. His infinite love is more than any of us can handle. Divine Love is a pure gift and we're all unworthy of it. So put aside any thoughts of worry about being worthy.

One last point: love demands freedom. There are no love-slaves in heaven. No one can enter the Kingdom of Heaven unless they yearn to enter, unless they have an ardent desire to be home at last with God, the Love of their life.

I've written this article to help cope with self-doubt. Don't ever say, "There must be something wrong with me," because of your separation anxiety. You're a normal human being, just a little home-sick, and that's not a big deal.

May the Lord be your strength and your joy.

PENTECOST AND YOU

By Fr. John T. Catoir, JCD | January 9, 2020

We celebrate the birthday of the Church on Pentecost Sunday fifty days after Easter. The Holy Spirit came upon the Apostles and transformed them from the frightened men they had become after the crucifixion into the courageous Apostles of Jesus Christ who fearlessly faced martyrdom.

At every Confirmation ceremony, the Bishop invokes the same Holy Spirit with these words: "All powerful Father, send your Holy Spirit upon them to be their helper and guide. Give them wisdom, strength and understanding...We ask this through Christ Our Lord, Amen."

If you want to benefit fully from these supernatural gifts, you must understand the importance of will training. Grace builds on nature. There is a door between you and the Holy Spirit, but you must open it. To deepen your trust and eliminate all doubt, you must will it.

Doubt is the enemy of trust. It will cloud your mind and undermine your best intentions. Doubt says, "This is too good to be true." Immediately reject all doubts because they will severely weaken your faith. A strong faith in the promises of Christ demands the full consent of your will.

The will has only one function: to say yes or no. Saying "maybe" is not an option. When you receive supernatural graces, you go beyond the natural order. When the Holy Spirit comes into your soul, He is giving you something that is objective and real; namely – His strength, His love, His joy, and His peace.

When Jesus says, "Be not afraid. I have come to save you, not to condemn you," a holy person listens to His words and accepts them as the absolute truth. Jesus is expressing His love. He is telling you that your peace of mind is very important to Him. Jesus means it when He says, "Be not afraid." Turn off fear and needless worry. Align yourself with God's will and accept His love with a grateful heart.

Jesus instituted all the Sacraments of the Church to help you through life. In the Sacrament of Reconciliation, He gives you the chance to rid yourself of guilt. Normally, if you are suffering from guilt and go to confession, you will feel immediate relief from the priest's absolution. However, some people linger in guilt and need special help.

The key is in the will to banish all doubt about God's infinite mercy. God wants your joy to be full. He wants you to make a fresh start. There is no sin too evil for His infinite mercy. After you receive absolution, you must decide that you are forgiven. Feelings to the contrary are not facts. Use your will power and terminate all doubt. That's faith in action. Refuse to wallow in fear and worry.

Take responsibility for your own happiness. Train your will to say, "Yes Lord, I believe. I trust your mercy with my whole heart." Even if the guilt comes back from time to time, reject it in all its forms. Go against your feelings. Make an act of faith. Thank the Lord again and again for His Mercy.

A rich and joyful life depends on how well you train your will to control your thoughts by rejecting all doubt. Decide to protect your present moment from needless worry and always put your faith above your feelings.

Once you understand and accept the importance of will-training, you will gradually feel the joy of His supernatural peace abiding in you.

May God bless you, always and forever.

POPE FRANCIS

By Fr. John T. Catoir, JCD | February 27, 2018

Pope Francis has my admiration because I hear the voice of love speaking through him. He always stresses God's infinite mercy.

Recently, a ninety-three-year-old atheist accused him of denying the existence of hell. This man who has nothing but contempt for Christianity, delighted in causing an uproar. The Pope denied his claim as a bogus reconstruction of what he misheard. The Pope's denial is good enough for me.

One thing is certain from what the Pope said: anyone who commits mortal sins and dies unrepentant does not enter the Kingdom of Heaven. Purgatory exists for those who receive mercy because of some excusing causes like ignorance and/or human weakness. Nevertheless, until their sins are washed away by their repentance, they cannot enter Heaven.

"God so loved the world…He sent his only begotten Son not to condemn it, but to save it." (John 3:16-17). Mercy seems like laxity to those who became alarmed when Pope Francis urged Catholics to rely more on their conscience in resolving personal moral issues.

Affirming freedom of conscience is an act of intellectual honesty and a way of being both merciful and understanding. These are God-like qualities.

Very few annulments were granted in the 1960s and 70s because of canonical rigidity. When Pope Francis was elected, it wasn't long before he began urging Catholics to rely more on their consciences, and that was music to my ears. Reliance on conscience is a long-established principle of Moral Theology.

Father Federico Lombardi, the Vatican spokesperson at the time, reported that Pope Francis was saying that in grave situations a well-formed conscience can be relied upon. The responsibility and gravity of the situation was to be determined by the parties themselves.

On July 29, 2013, he said, "If someone is gay, and sincerely searches for the Lord, and has good will – who am I to judge?" He immediately received a flood of criticism for that quote, but the parents of gay children felt genuine solace. While he did not endorse same sex marriage, he did say there could be some sort of civil union to protect their civil rights. He opposes promiscuity in general.

Conservative Catholics are usually fearful that any relaxation of the laws pertaining to marriage and divorce and contraception would threaten the Church's broader stance on medical ethics and sexual issues. This is an understandable concern, but not an insurmountable one. Freedom of conscience is a human right. Granted, it can be abused, but it must be protected. Every right can be abused.

Pope Paul VI affirmed the immoral nature of artificial contraception in his Encyclical, *Humanae Vitae*. Pope Francis is preparing for the canonization of Pope Paul, and he has remained firm in his opposition to those who refuse to have children because it interferes with their lifestyle. Nevertheless, he respects the consciences of those who are struggling to find the strength to raise children in today's world.

Pope Francis agrees with the various National Hierarchies who have instructed the laity that they may use private conscience in resolving these matters. He also highlighted Paul VI's instruction to priests, urging them to show compassion in the confessional in matters involving human weakness.

What I admire most about Pope Francis are his Christ-like qualities: humility, compassion, and kindness.

May the Lord be your strength and your joy.

PREPARE YOUR HEART FOR HOLINESS

By Fr. John T. Catoir, JCD | May 18, 2017

Uniting with the suffering of Christ is a tradition and a Lenten devotion done for the remission of one's sins, the increase of grace, and the salvation of souls. Try meditating on it for one minute a day as we approach Good Friday. At least read this column once. A prophecy from the Hebrew Bible was fulfilled that day on Calvary, "By His wounds we are healed." (Isaiah 53:5)

Jesus sweat blood during His agony in the Garden. "His sweat became like great drops of blood falling down on the ground." (Luke 22:44) This is a rare medical condition called hematidrosis, where severe stress causes the capillaries to break down, and blood enters the sweat glands.

One shudders at the thought that Christ laid down His life for us. The degree of His suffering is beyond imagination, and yet it was a true historical event. "They shouted 'crucify Him'," (Mark 15:12), and Pontius Pilate condemned Him to death by crucifixion. Some skeptics have claimed that His death was a hoax, and that all those who claimed that He rose from the dead were frauds and liars.

Nothing is further from the truth. No one ever survived a Roman death sentence. A crucifixion was always preceded by humiliating tortures. The scourging at the pillar was calculated to advance the process of the victim's death by massive hemorrhaging. The flagellation consisted of at least 39 lashes from whips of braided leather with pieces of sharp stones inserted in the strands in order to rip the flesh from the bones.

Many victims of a Roman scourging suffered the loss of so much blood that they died before it was over. In the case of Jesus, after they spit on Him and insulted Him, a crown of thorns was pressed into His skull and they dragged Him to His feet. Exhausted and bleeding profusely, He was forced to carry that heavy weight as, "They led Him away to crucify Him..." (Matthew 27:31)

On the way, He saw His grieving mother. Scripture was fulfilled in her that day, "A sword of sorrow will pierce your soul," (Luke 2:34) She walked along with the procession accompanied by a group of devoted women. Jesus said to them, "Daughters of Jerusalem. Do not weep for Me." (Luke 23:28) "I am leaving the world and am returning to the Father." (John 16:28)

Reaching the top of Calvary, they stripped Him of His garments and, "Cast lots for His clothing." (Psalm 22:18) Then they drove spikes into His hands and feet, nailing Him to the cross.

A song from our liturgy reminds us of Mary during the three hours of His agony. "At the cross her station keeping, stood the mournful Mother weeping." A Roman soldier moved forward to pierce His heart with a sword. Jesus cried out with a loud voice, "Father, into your hands I commend My spirit." (Luke 23:46)

"They took the body of Jesus and wrapped it with spices in linen cloths." (John 19:40) And they buried Him in the tomb.

Pope Francis, Easter 2016: "To those who have lost hope and joy in life; to the elderly who struggle alone and feel their strength waning; to young people who seem to have no future; to everyone, I address these words of the Risen Lord: 'See, I am making all things new…to the thirsty, I give water as a gift from the spring of the water of life."

PRIVATE CONSCIENCE AND THE CHURCH

By Fr. John T. Catoir, JCD | October 21, 2017

The late Bishop Fulton Sheen explained that there are two kinds of truths: "Outer truths, which we master, like the distance of the sun from the earth; and inner truths, which master us, e.g., God is merciful to the penitent. Inner truths affect a person's destiny, like a vocational calling; they are matters of conscience."

In 1965, the Second Vatican Council defined conscience as "the most secret core and sanctuary of the person, where alone with God in one's innermost self, each one perceives the voice of God."

Now consider this: if a couple, after much prayer and sincere reflection considered themselves to be truly married in the eyes of God, but many others considered them to be living in sin, would you judge them to be sinners? Or would you give them the benefit of the doubt? Pope Francis once said, "Who am I to judge," and he disturbed a lot of people.

The Church has always taught the primacy of conscience. The law is the remote norm of morality, while the individual conscience is considered the proximate norm. This traditional teaching of moral theology has certain consequences; for instance, a law does not bind in conscience until the individual knows it exists, and until he or she accepts it as objectively true and morally binding. There is such a thing as licit dissent.

The American hierarchy issued a pastoral letter entitled "Human Life in Our Day," (November 15, 1968). Here is a pertinent excerpt: "There exists in the Church a lawful freedom of inquiry, of thought, and general norms of licit dissent... In the final analysis, no person is to be forced to act in a manner contrary to his/her conscience, as the moral tradition of the Church attests."

In doubtful matters, Catholics should be guided by the teaching authority of the Church, which is referred to as the Magisterium. What exactly does that mean? At the 1991 workshop for the hierarchy, theologian Avery Dulles, S.J., who later became a Cardinal, explained it this way: "The Magisterium is one, but only one informant of conscience. In matters of individual conscience, Catholics have the right to examine all available information in forming their conscience." This teaching is not new.

There has always been an emphasis on God's mercy in the teaching of the Church. Jesus said, "Go and learn what this means, I desire mercy, not sacrifice." (Matthew 9:13)

"For God did not send his Son into the world to condemn the world, but to save the world through Him." (John 3:17)

Pope Francis has been emphasizing mercy quite a bit. To some, he seems to be breaking the rules. The truth is he has been manifesting the Spirit of Jesus who excoriated the Pharisees of old. Here's what Jesus said, "And you experts in the law, woe to you, because you load people down with burdens they can hardly carry and you will not lift a finger to help them." (Luke 11:46)

The Pope's canonical critics demand greater rigidity. Are they wise? I think not. In view of the fact that Jesus issued this command: "Judge not that you be not judged," wouldn't it make more sense if these papal critics calmed down, and left the matter of judging souls to God.

Divine Mercy is something we're all going to need one day. Better to be safe than sorry.

May the Lord be your strength and your joy.

PROUD TO BE A CATHOLIC PRIEST
By Fr. John T. Catoir, JCD | June 10, 2013

The privilege of being a priest hit me powerfully recently. I was part of an assembly of priests who gathered to celebrate their respective ordination anniversaries at a concelebrated mass.

(Photo: Dale Dexter)

Priests serve all over the world. *Salute Magazine* recently had a cover of 13 smiling Catholic Chaplains in their fatigue uniforms. They help the 16,500 Catholic service men and woman currently deployed in Afghanistan. As I looked at those brave men, I remembered how my own vocation came while I was serving as an MP in the Army. Then I thought about the hundreds of chaplains who have died in combat over the years.

Did you know that 2,700 priests were burned in the ovens at Dachau during World War II? They opposed Hitler's mad scheme to annihilate the Jews. Father William O'Malley, S.J. has a new book about it. (Note: he can be located at Seattle University, 924 E. Cherry St., Washington, 98122).

One priest who managed to escape the Nazi reign of terror was Msgr. John Oesterreicher, a convert from Judaism, who founded the Institute of Judeo-Christian Studies at Seton Hall University in New Jersey. He opposed Hitler openly in the late 30s, but miraculously escaped to America in 1940.

Did you know that there were two Catholic chaplains who received the Congressional Medal of Honor? Father (Navy Captain) Joseph O'Callahan (died in1964), and Father (Lieutenant) Vincent Capodanno (died in 1967), a Maryknoll priest who volunteered to serve in a Vietnam combat zone.

Their deaths reminded me of my friend Father Mychal Judge, the Franciscan NYC Fire Department chaplain who died as a first responder in the 9/11 Twin Tower tragedy. Priests all over the world are giving up their lives for others every day.

Bishop James Walsh, the founder of the Maryknoll Missionary Society, wrote, "The task of a missionary is to go to a place where he is not wanted, but is needed, and to remain there until he is no longer needed, but is wanted."

Salesian Father Alfred Marzo, who recently celebrated 50 years of priestly service to the poor in India, said, "I am the happiest man alive." A life of altruism does that to a man. He performed his normal pastoral duties every single day, but also helped build a pipeline to bring clean water to their village. He even taught them to construct a strong foot bridge to save his people from being washed away during the monsoon season.

Not long ago, we had our own monsoon season in the form of that shameful pedophile scandal. Did you ever hear the joke about lawyers? "It's the 98% that gives the rest of them a bad name." (Forgive me, I'm a lawyer myself.) With the priesthood, it was just the opposite. The two percent that gave the rest of us a bad name. Always remember that it was a repentant thief who was the first one to enter the Kingdom of Heaven.

Today, there are nearly a half-million priests in the world, serving in remote towns and villages, in wealthy parishes, and everywhere in between. They bring Christ's light and love to our troubled world. Granted, we have our domineering egotists and our alcoholics, nevertheless I am still proud to have served the Lord as a Catholic priest for over 53 years.

Pope Francis recently included himself when he said, "Pray for us priests, we are men, we are human, and we are tempted." Amen to that.

REJOICING ALWAYS IS POSSIBLE

By Fr. John T. Catoir, JCD | April 23, 2017

Having just gone through Lent and Easter, we've seen the stark reality of the cross followed by the glorious manifestation of the resurrection. We are now living in the joyful season of Easter. But I ask you, is it realistic to ask anyone to be joyful in this crazy world of ours? The answer is a definite YES!

There will always be crosses, and yet we are called to live joyfully through all the drudgery and pain of life. We all suffer physical and emotional pain of one kind or another: our bodies ache, people disappoint, financial woes engender fear, the possibility of war persists, but despite this, we are still called to live joyfully.

St. Paul, who suffered mightily in his day, urged us to rejoice always because of the knowledge of God's love. How do we know that God loves us? We know it by faith. Jesus Christ told us to call God "Our Father." Doesn't every father want his children to be happy? That's why St. Paul said, "Rejoice always, and be grateful in all circumstances, for this is the will of God for you in Christ Jesus", (I Cor. 5: 16). He took this magnificent idea from Jesus, who at the last supper said, "I have told you all these things that My joy may be in you, and your joy may be complete," (John 15:11).

Forgive me if I repeat this theme again and again, but my readers urge me to keep it up. I appeal to Pope John Paul II for confirmation. He wrote, "Christ came to bring joy, joy to children, joy to parents, joy to families and friends, joy to workers and scholars, joy to the sick and elderly, joy to all humanity. In a true sense, joy is the keynote message and the recurring motif of the Gospels...Go therefore and become messengers of joy."

Our response ought to be, "Yes, I will Lord. I will be glad, and filled with joy because of You." (Psalm 9:2) But too often we fall short of our high calling. Recently Bishop Robert Barron wrote about the strict moral code that the Church proclaims in matters of sexuality. The reason we push for excellence in every area of human life is because the Church exists to create saints. Many Catholics say the Church should scale back on these rigid standards, but Christ calls us higher. Jesus said, "Be ye perfect."(Matthew 5:48) We all know the heartbreak and suffering that comes from unbridled sexuality. Mediocrity and irresponsibility always lead to misery and death.

Of course we are weak and sinful. Of course we need Divine mercy just to survive spiritually from day to day, but we also need Christian ideals that call us to nobility and holiness. Mediocrity is not an option.

"Rejoice always," is a call to perfection. We need to accept spiritual joy as a realistic goal. When Jesus told us to, "Love one another as I have loved you," he knew it would involve the cross. Wherever there is love there is service, wherever there is service there is sacrifice, and wherever there is sacrifice there is the cross. Joy and the cross are not contradictory; they are, in fact, complimentary. Jesus knew that the only way to find true joy was by emptying oneself in loving service.

"The greatest honor you can give to Almighty God is to live joyfully because of the knowledge of his love." – Julian of Norwich

RICH MAN, POOR MAN

By Fr. John T. Catoir, JCD | June 8, 2017

The balance between economics and spirituality is a delicate matter worth your earnest consideration. I am guided by Jesus Christ as I attempt to make sense out of today's world. I hope this article will be of help to you as you think about the future.

There has always been tension between the rich and the poor. One hundred years ago, the Communist revolution exploded in Russia. It was based on the Marxian theory that economic equality could be regulated by the state. After millions of murders by Communist tyrants, thousands of Communist multi-millionaires abound in the world. What a waste!

In 1776, the new nation of America adopted its Declaration of Independence declaring that all men and women were created equal. Two years later, after numerous peasant revolts, the French National Assembly abolished feudalism in France sweeping away the right to personal serfdom, which was the European form of slavery.

Leading up to these revolutions, for thousands of years, landowners, royal personages, and political tyrants amassed fortunes while the peasant classes labored in abject poverty. It has always been part of the human condition.

Many of the poor came to believe that God had abandoned them and who could blame them. But Jesus warned the rich about being too selfish and too self-satisfied. He warned both the rich and poor alike against self-centeredness and greed.

He said, "Blessed are the poor in spirit," but He never condemned the rich as such. For that matter, He never condemned any class of people. What he did reject was the idea that wealth and social status was a sign of God's favor. Very often, just the opposite is true.

Jesus said, "Blessed are the poor in spirit." The poor in spirit are those who put God's will before their own; those who strive to please the Lord God every day of their lives. True holiness is found among both the rich and the poor, but not necessarily on an equal basis.

Jesus reminds every one of us that, "We know not the day nor the hour." (Matthew 25:13) Scientific progress in the last century has been spectacular, but all our cell phones, computers, and fancy watches will never tell us the exact day we will be called to judgment by our Heavenly Father.

Our country is divided today, not so much between the haves and the have nots, as in the past, but between those who want a Nanny State, and those who don't.

God helps those who help themselves. In nature, all the animals know they need to work to feed themselves. If they want to stay alive, the natural law demands this of them.

Apart from any of these economic issues, what we all need is peace of soul. Finding peace within ourselves is a matter of grace, prayer, and obedience to God's will. I leave you with this blessing to help you along the way.

"May the passion of our Lord Jesus Christ, the merits of Our Blessed Virgin Mary, and all the saints, and whatsoever good you do, or suffering you endure, may it bring about the remission of your sins, the increase of grace, and the gift of everlasting life. Amen."

SADNESS

By Fr. John T. Catoir, JCD | February 7, 2018

When I was little, I was sad because my parents wouldn't buy me a pony. (We lived in an apartment.) When I was a teen, I was sad because I had pimples. As an adult, I became sad when I started losing my hair. You might say, sadness is part of the human condition.

However, there are more serious kinds of sadness. The ones that have to do with our spirituality. I recently received this letter from a reader:

"Father, why is it that lately, when I pray, I feel like it's very rote and flat. Although my prayers come from the heart and I have a strong faith, it's not the same as it once was. It makes me feel very sad. I never have serious doubts, but I feel I can never measure up."

I understand this kind of sadness very well. I've had my share of it over the years. It's a nostalgia over the loss of something or someone dear to you. Feeling down or unhappy because of grief or disappointment is very human.

When I was in the seminary, I prayed so hard that my mother would live to see me ordained. She suffered for years from many ailments. I trusted God, and prayed that she'd make it, but alas, she died a year before my ordination.

The normal grief period was compounded by my doubts about God's love. I believed I was called to be a priest, but new doubts flooded my mind. What if my vocation was a creation of my imagination? If God really loved me, why didn't He answer my prayers? What if I fail as a priest?

It was my dark night of the soul. I lived through it by sheer will power. The pious feelings that brought me from the Army to the seminary had evaporated. Nevertheless, I persevered.

Despite that painful year, I recovered and was ordained on May 28th, 1960. It was a joyful day, but the grief was still lingering. My Dad and I had a good cry, and then life went on. I never looked back and I never doubted my vocation again.

What if I had given in to those fears and dropped out. As a priest over the years, I've touched many lives through my work in the parish, through the written word (writing is a vocation within a vocation), and through my nationally syndicated TV Show, *Christopher Close-up*. I'm happy now that I didn't allow my sadness to deter me from enjoying my life as a priest.

To all of you who are suffering from one nagging sadness or another, if it has caused you to believe that God has withdrawn His consolation from you because you are no longer as pleasing to Him as you once were, let me tell you emphatically: THAT IS SIMPLY NOT TRUE!

Feelings are not facts. Only faith can give you the facts about your relationship with God. God is unchanging love. He loves you on good days and bad, during good seasons and sad. Carry on with courage! Know that the merits of your actions increase when you're not doing it for emotional gratification. But for the love of God.

When your sadness passes away, you'll see that it was a gift from God to help you bear rich and abundant good fruit for all eternity.

May the Lord be your strength and your joy as you journey through life, with all its sad moments.

SCHOOL SHOOTINGS
By Fr. John T. Catoir, JCD | May 25, 2018

When plane hijacking became a national threat, we immediately addressed the problem by upgrading preventive measures at our airports. X-Ray surveillance, body searches, luggage inspections were all resisted at first, but these stricter methods worked. The immediate public reaction was to complain: it's too invasive, too time-consuming, too annoying, etc. But now people feel safer, and the threat of hijackings is no longer on everyone's mind.

We need to do the same thing for our children who are terrified by the mass murders at schools. We need to upgrade our surveillance techniques. The problem needs to be addressed from a two-pronged perspective: 1.Tighter prevention measures are needed against outside intruders: metal detectors, armed guards, etc., and 2. Increased mental health vigilance must be introduced. Too many suicidal youngsters have access to unsecured firearms. How can a person raging with enough hatred to commit mass murder be, at the same time, sweet and innocent looking to one and all? Most parents know when they have a troubled child; maybe not a mass murderer, but a potential problem. We must turn to the parents more for their cooperation.

To the trained eye, the normality or abnormality of a person can be surmised. Right now there is too little emphasis on the students. Many of these atrocities have been committed by students with mental health issues. This is a spiritual problem more than a gun control issue. Too much emphasis has been placed on the moment of combat, and not enough on the remote cause, the brooding dysfunctional killer lurking in the shadows.

This must change! I've tweeted about this problem, but none of my critics offered adequate solutions. The most serious objection was concern over the constitutionality of any invasion of privacy. That's what they said about airport searches. My answer is simple: take only those measures that are constitutional. Cooperating parents can tell us a lot. Refusal to cooperate might be a wake-up call. Some homes are virtual arsenals. Safety measures need to be secure. Can these homes be identified without violating the Constitution?

All lawmakers should be concerned about the common good. Teddy Roosevelt insisted that the Constitution was made for the people, not the people for the Constitution. Our children are terrified by the fear of being murdered at school. We are failing them if we do nothing more than fight to ban guns. The second amendment is not the issue. This is a spiritual and a mental health problem. We need just laws to protect us against disasters. Also, people who have arsenals in their homes should be subject to legal inspections. We owe our teenagers respect enough to make their safety a top priority.

I know how much harm a demonic presence can do. I ran a drug and alcohol rehabilitation for a few years. All of our clients were struggling with their own demons, and they weren't afraid to admit it. A demonic influence is part of the mental health issue. I'm calling upon all police departments and federal law enforcement agencies to flush out potential killers by upgrading their preventive measures against school shootings. Working within the letter of the law, you can make a difference. Lives can be saved by fostering a spirit of cooperation among all concerned.

May God protect you always and may the Lord be your strength and your joy.

SCIENCE AND WISDOM

By Fr. John T. Catoir, JCD | December 15, 2017

According to Google, science is defined as a branch of knowledge acquired through observation and experimentation. Wisdom is defined as the quality of having knowledge and good judgment.

A scientist can lack all knowledge about the soul and the spiritual life while a philosopher can lack all the knowledge needed to build a computer, but it takes wisdom to know which of these two forms of knowledge is more important in the long run.

Atheistic scientists say there is not a shred of evidence in the entire universe for the existence of the supernatural. Albert Einstein, using deductive reasoning, said that there must be a Supreme Intelligence behind the universe. Einstein's view is almost universally preferred.

Atheistic scientists are very limited. They engage in the systematic study of the structure and behavior of things animate and inanimate in the natural world. They do this through observation and experimentation. This preoccupation with the world leaves them little time to ponder the things of the Spirit. It is a scientific fact that the earliest humans believed in an afterlife. However, modern science rules out the possibility of life beyond death. Is that wise?

At times, scientists are very helpful in supplying us with an educated opinion on important matters. For instance, 30,000 scientists recently signed a statement that "there is no scientific consensus that human activity is the cause of climate change." Some questioned whether this was a wise statement, but it certainly is the scientific outlook of a considerable number of professional scientists.

Agnostics doubt God's existence. Most of them refuse to be bound by any religious principles. George Washington said that every society needs to follow religious principles in order to survive. By promoting unfettered freedom, we end up with an opioid epidemic; our drug subculture that has destroyed millions of lives. Is it wise to ignore what we see is happening before our eyes?

America was heading in the direction of globalism, where a country surrenders its sovereignty to international law. The proponents of globalism lacked the wisdom to see its negative economic consequences. American voters had the sagacity to challenge this movement before it blossomed into a nightmare.

A lack of wisdom can be a dangerous thing. St. Paul wrote in Hebrews 10:36, "You need endurance, so that you may receive the joy that Jesus promised those who do the will of God." It takes wisdom to discern the truth that we need to live in harmony with God's will. This is done by following Jesus and the Golden Rule: "Do unto others as you would have them to do unto you."

All law can be traced to the Supreme Law: "Love God, and love your neighbor as you love yourself." This wisdom has come to us directly from Divine Revelation, and it appeals to right reason. Wisdom is the ground of our being and life.

All the religions of the world agree that God exists, God is benign, God has a plan, God wants us to love one another, and God invites us to join Him one day in heaven after living a good life here on earth. He respects our freedom and will allow us to decline His invitation if we so choose. I suggest that you put on the will to be obedient to God's plan for you, and enjoy your precious life both here and hereafter.

Always ask the Lord to give you the strength you need to discern the difference between wisdom and science.

SECURING OUR BORDERS

By Fr. John T. Catoir, JCD | April 23, 2017

Protecting our borders is a matter of justice. Pope Francis made a good point when he said "Every nation has the right to secure its own borders." He also expressed serious concern over the plight of the refugees in the Middle East and Europe. He is encouraging all nations to be merciful as they formulate their immigration policies.

It's important that we respect both of his concerns.

What worries me is the way the American hierarchy is presenting the Pope's thinking on these two issues. The idea of being generous in receiving immigrants does not cancel the nation's right to be very cautious in the screening process. Those who are trying to enter the U.S. are not all angels. Many immigrants in the past have said "Death to America" under their breath.

The serious danger of exposing innocent civilians to the deadly attacks of Jihadist terrorists cannot be overestimated. We see the malice involved and the suffering it causes.

The laity is reacting to recent letters of the hierarchy with dismay. Here is a typical example.

"The outcry from U.S. Church leaders against the President's vetting of immigrants, saying they "strongly disagree" contains more emotion than common sense. They fail to mention that these screening actions attempt to protect citizens from jihadist terrorists who blatantly told us they are going to infiltrate the refugees."– Rich Matrisciano, Andover, New Jersey in a letter to the editor of The Beacon, February 16, 2017.

America allows into our country approximately a million people a year, which is about twice as many as the next largest number. Some of them are on temporary visas, but they all have to be vetted.

The Holy Father has never criticized any particular country for its immigration policies. For instance, Mexico regards illegal entry to their nation as a felony crime punishable immediately by a two-year prison term. To me that seems harsh. America sends illegal felons back to their own country.

This is not only right and just, it's a necessity if we are to protect our people from potential danger. The fact that some Bishops said they "strongly disagree" with our national security concerns seems to show an insensitivity to the legitimate fears of millions of Americans. We've seen too many ruthless attacks to be lax about our border security.

I fear that many Catholics might think that we treat the matter of border control too lightly. Interpreting the words of any pope must be done carefully. We can and we should follow our Holy Father Pope Francis on both issues: Protect our borders effectively and at the same time, be merciful to the many innocent victims of terrorism who have suffered so very much.

God bless one and all. May the Lord be your strength and our joy.

SELF-HELP IS A CHOICE

By Fr. John T. Catoir, JCD | May 6, 2017

One of the most important things you can do to improve your mental health and strengthen your spiritual life is to find a way to fill your mind with uplifting thoughts, because the thoughts you wallow in today will always filter down into your feelings tomorrow. Terminate panic, eliminate self-pity, and focus on joy.

Uplifting spiritual thoughts will liberate you from a good bit of mental misery. Toxic thoughts, on the other hand, will always make you feel sad. So much emotional pain is the direct result of fear. But Jesus said, "Fear is useless; what you need is trust."

We all know that you can reduce negativity by the simple act of counting your blessings. Make a habit of filling your mind with uplifting ideas. Jesus said, "In this world you will have many troubles, but take heart and cheer up, for I have overcome the world".

Everyone has the power to change the bad habit of being gloomy. Dorothy Day called it the "duty of delight". But how do you do it? Follow me closely on this. The mind only has room for one set of thoughts at a time. If you decide to think good thoughts, the toxic ones will have no room to fester.

Healing can begin the minute you decide to move out of the self-imposed mental swamp that drags you down. You can't be discouraged if it takes a bit of time. Gaining control is like turning off the furnace of an over-heated building. The furnace may be off but the heat only fades away gradually.

Here's another mental trick. Do not identify with your thoughts. You are not your thoughts. You are the observer of your thoughts. A suicidal obsession is an evil intruder. Cast it out! When you start slipping into a dark state of mind, stop it. Say NO! Dis-identify with those negative thoughts.

You are a child of God, destined for an eternity of happiness in heaven. Live your life by faith. Don't give in to morbid sulking. Terminate that lazy mental discipline which steals your joy.

Holding on to hurtful thoughts will only perpetuate the pain. Therefore, reject sad ideas – especially memories that make you cry.

Cast them aside. The will says 'yes' or 'no'. Do not let the past drag you down.

I've been writing books on this subject for over 35 years, and I'm still working on it, so I know it won't be easy. But the need for mental discipline is acknowledged by every religion in the world and by science as well. Persevere! Faith can make a difference. Turn to the Lord and ask for help. You are never alone. God is right there helping you every step of the way.

Poisonous thoughts will hang around only when you do nothing to dispel them. Pray for the grace to live in the present moment. Instead of wallowing in the past or worrying about the future, let your eyes, your ears, and all your senses do the work for you.

Good music can rock you out of a funk. I prefer Dave Brubeck, but I enjoyed the hard rock band 'Shinedown'. Their song *Be a Simple Man* touched me. Here are a few lyrics: "Take your time, be a simple man, don't live too fast. Find love and don't forget the One above." Ah yes, wisdom comes from many sources.

May the Lord be your strength and your joy.

SEXUALITY

By Fr. John T. Catoir, JCD | June 23, 2018

We all need to understand our own sexuality – and there's a lot to learn. If you want to have a peaceful and meaningful life, it would be wise not to allow yourself to be taken in completely by the surrounding culture of sexual freedom.

The men and women we see on TV dramas and comedies are for the most part, living promiscuous lives, and it shows. Most of them— even in the comedies—are unhappy, depressed, frustrated, frightened, and often filled with rage. Lacking any spiritual depth, they are doomed to ongoing misery because they have not yet found their true home. "Our hearts are restless, until they rest in Thee O Lord." – St. Augustine.

Self-control is a dirty word in our sexually liberated world because it requires wisdom, strength, and will power. Understanding God is necessary for finding peace and happiness. Jesus came, "That your joy may be full." Disbelieve that at your own risk. God wants those who are called to marriage to find a mate who will offer them the hope of a lasting bond of mutual love. He wants them to enjoy a cheerful home with loving children. This requires many skills that go into the creation of an environment of emotional comfort. A background of faith and spirituality will help to make all your dreams come true.

Let's take a moment to examine how men and women are pro- grammed. A man instinctively moves from attraction to sex to love. He wants what he wants. Hopefully he learns that one-night stands lead nowhere. Women, on the other hand, are more intuitive. They move from attraction to love to sex. They have a deeper understanding of the fact that to live a happy life, they will need to attract a good man and demand his respect. Their future depends on it.

Men, in general, are as good as the woman in their lives. A man is instinctively looking for a woman who will be faithful to him and help him to build a family. The long-range consequences of a promis- cuous youth will weaken your self-control. Everyone needs a genuine spiritual life to be able to make a strong commitment to fidelity in marriage. Think ahead! Good men and women do not want to be promiscuous; it goes against the highest values of the human spirit. Human weakness however often leads to the neglect of one's spiritual life and the loss of self-control.

In the old days, mothers taught their daughters to be careful about the way they dressed, and for good reason. To show up at a party immodestly dressed where young men are drinking is a formula for danger with lasting consequences. Those who scoff at Mom's old-fashioned ideas often pay a high price. The dismal statistics are in on the sexual revolution.

The divorce rate has nearly doubled and one third of all children born in America are born to single mothers. This has led to much misery, economic insecurity, and in many cases, life-long poverty. The chance for a good education is also lost to many children while psychological problems abound. Drugs and alcohol abuse is sky-rocketing, along with teen suicides. So beware my dear men and women.

The prevailing culture of sexual freedom can destroy your life if you let it. A word to the wise is sufficient.

May the Lord be your strength and your joy.

SIR WINSTON CHURCHILL
By Fr. John T. Catoir, JCD | January 18, 2018

The late Prime Minister of Great Britain, Sir Winston Churchill, has been called the greatest person of the twentieth century. His personal courage inspired his nation and the world to triumph over the military might of the Nazi regime. Adolf Hitler, the tyrant who set out to dominate the world, surrendered and later committed suicide in a Berlin bunker.

Churchill was victorious as he said he would be. He was a great leader. But great leaders are not necessarily perfect human beings. He drank too much, he was coarse and crude. He called the German leader – 'Shitler.'

He had many women critics who considered him a man of poor taste. Bessie Braddock wrote, "Winston, you're a disgusting drunk." He replied, "Bessie my dear, you are ugly and disgusting, but I shall be sober tomorrow and you will still be ugly and disgusting."

Another critic, Lady Nancy Astor wrote, "Winston, if you were my husband, I would poison your coffee." He replied, "Nancy, if you were my wife I would drink it."

But he had real opposition from within his own party. Those who feared losing the war wanted to appease Hitler and make a deal to avoid the loss of life. Churchill, with a will of iron, screamed, "WE SHALL NEVER SURRENDER!" It was a cry that became a national mantra.

Speaking to his own unruly Parliament, he would shout at the top of his lungs, "Do you want to see the Nazi Swastika flying over Buckingham Palace?!" "NEVER!", they shouted back. "NEVER!"

The Darkest Hour is a wonderful film that depicted Winston at his weakest. Overwhelmed by superior Nazi forces and fiercely opposed by some within his own party, Churchill, instead of caving in, stood tall and fought back.

He ordered a flotilla of private yachts into service to sail out and save the British troops stranded on the beaches of Dunkirk. The generals scoffed at the idea, 'It would take a miracle." The politicians, all afraid of German bombers, thought Sir Winston had gone mad.

But he persisted with the order – and heaven cooperated. The weather was cloudy which prevented the German Air Force from attacking. And so from May 26th to June 4th, 1940, a fleet of 850 boats crossed the Channel, and successfully brought back more than 338,000 British and French troops. It was considered a miracle.

Churchill, a chronic cigar smoker, was elated as he lit up and had a stiff drink. He suffered the ordinary ailments of aging, however. He was overweight and arthritic and the film showed that his emotional life was not entirely free of self-doubt and fear.

But always true to himself, he brushed aside all the negativity and bravely continued to chant his battle cry: "Victory at any cost!" Churchill successfully changed the course of history.

There are many times in history when God intervenes. This was one of the most important. The outcome of World War II was much improved by the weather. Many believers saw it as God's response to the faith and courage of a prayerful people.

It's important for us to take inspiration from the courage of great leaders. By the grace of God, all things are possible. If you stick to your goals, with the help of God, you will be grateful for all eternity.

May the Lord be your strength and your joy.

SOME FEAR IS SALUTARY

By Fr. John T. Catoir, JCD | May 22, 2017

A woman wrote to me recently: "Father I was wondering if you could offer me some suggestions? I am trying to trust in Our Lord but I tend to be anxious, sometimes to the point of having anxiety attacks. I want to trust God, but I get so frightened."

I answered her quickly, St. Thomas More once wrote, "Do not be anxious because you're anxious." He was saying that some fear is normal. Coping with severe fear may be another matter, where you need professional help. But even Jesus suffered the agony in the Garden.

Jesus trusted His Father, but he was human enough to experience fear. It wasn't death itself he feared, but he did fear the way He was going to die. We all must accept the fact that to fear is human.

Sometimes our fears are salutary. John Newton, the man who wrote the great hymn *Amazing Grace,* was a slave-trader who converted to Christ out of fear for his salvation. Here is how he expressed it, "T'was grace that taught my heart to fear, and grace my fears relieved." Some fear is designed to help you to regain your senses.

Sometimes the lack of fear can be a problem. Those who manage financial markets are worried that the lack of fear in today's investors can lead to serious problems. At this writing, the bull market is raging; investors seem to have lost sight of the big picture.

James Macintosh wrote in the *Wall Street Journal* (May 16, 2017), "The fearlessness of today's investors can be compared to picking up pennies in front of a steamroller." For instance, in caring for your soul, it's not wise to ignore the odds. The world is full of danger and temptation.

There are 570,000 drug-related deaths every year. Dabbling with pot has led many users to try more serious drugs. The unlucky ones have ended up insane or dead.

We need more prudence and wisdom in caring for our souls. A spirit of laxity has invaded the souls of many. People are more willing to move toward the slippery slope where so many have fallen to their doom.

Church leaders are beginning to worry about Sunday Mass attendance. The New York Archdiocese has reported a drop of nearly 20% in the past few years. This is a nationwide trend.

The fear of committing a mortal sin once motivated many Catholics to make the sacrifices needed to remain faithful to the worship of God. Today, a lack of any fear seems to be having the exact opposite effect.

A prolonged drifting away from the discipline of practicing one's faith often leads to a loss of the spirit of reverence, and in some cases, ends in a complete falling away from the Church.

Purging ourselves of an excess of religious scruples can be a good thing. Jesus said, "Be not anxious." He wanted his people to be motivated by love rather than fear.

But there is a more salutary fear that should always remain with us; namely, the fear of displeasing God. The spirit of reverence should never be abandoned.

May the Lord be your strength and your joy.

SPIRITUAL JOY THROUGH DAYDREAMING

By Fr. John T. Catoir, JCD | August 10, 2018

St. Ignatius Loyola, the founder of the Jesuits, explains how God often communicates with us: "Good discernment consists of prayerfully pondering the great desires that well up in our daydreams."

Our daydreams are often God's way of communication with us. God enflames our hearts with holy desires. Some come in the form of an attraction toward a life of service. Sometimes it has to do with our vocation. Often it has to do with the choice of volunteering for a noble cause. St. Ignatius speaks of prayerful daydreaming as a key to spiritual discernment.

Basically, the Holy Spirit speaks to us through holy desires encased in our daydreams. Actual grace is a light to the mind or an impulse to the will. Only gradually do we come to discern what God wants of us. At first, we may not fully understand whether this is a dream from God or not. When a daydream brings you peace and joy, it's a good sign that God is speaking to you.

There are many approaches to discernment in our Catholic tradition. My own vocation emerged from daydreaming about being a priest. At the time I was sure I wanted to marry and raise a family. Becoming a priest was the last thing I wanted, or so I thought. I resisted the idea strenuously for over five years, until I finally realized that the priesthood was what I wanted most of all. Spiritual directors have always known that the Holy Spirit often leads His children along paths they would not have chosen for themselves.

Many of my columns are written when I'm in a state of spiritual day-dreaming. Sometimes I receive the inspiration for an entire article all at once. I may be half asleep when I get up to scribble some notes so I can remember them later.

Here's a new article taken from notes that have been laying around for a few weeks. You can decide if it's a message from the Holy Spirit for you.

We. All. Need. Joy.

Just as we need air to breathe, we also need joy in our lives. There are so many miserable days. We need joy to lift us up. It's important to know that joy is more than a feeling. It's a kind of inner contentment based on the knowledge of God's unending love.

If you have chosen Jesus as your Lord and Savior, you already have His joy in your heart whether you feel it or not. You must learn to activate it by deciding to live joyfully because of your faith in God's love.

Never cut yourself off from spiritual joy or you will suffer from needless loneliness. The Gospels tell us that God is Love. Since joy is the by-product of love, it follows that God's presence brings both Love and Joy. The Kingdom of God is within you.

Accepting this truth opens us to an on-going participation in His Joy. If you are suffering from bad feelings or from some sorrow, you know that you always have Christ's joy abiding in you. Use it as a crutch when you need to.

At times sorrow will overcome you. No need to be afraid; it doesn't mean that The Lord has abandoned you. His Joy is always within you. Learn to claim it. That's how you can do what St. Paul urged us to do, namely, "Rejoice in all circumstances."

STAY CALM

By Fr. John T. Catoir, JCD | July 29, 2017

Robert Louis Stevenson wrote: "Most of us reflect our surroundings. However, men (and women) with quiet minds cannot be perplexed or frightened; they carry on in times of fortune or misfortune at their own private pace, like a clock during a thunderstorm."

I love that quote, but I must admit, I do not always have a 'quiet mind'. What's more, I have never aspired to operate like a clock. Thunderstorms will send me running for shelter, even though they never bother me when I'm indoors by a fireside. But when I get caught outdoors in a storm, staying calm is not an option.

It's human at times to be perplexed and frightened, especially when terrorists and hoodlums threaten your safety, or when your health has taken a turn for the worse. Though beset by human weakness, you always seem to maintain confidence in God's infinite protection and mercy.

Heavy burdens are placed on your shoulders every day and, yet, you manage to persevere because of God's grace. I'll tell you how this has worked out for me. There is something that has helped me get through many a storm. It's called 'Presence'.

This is a mystery that you, as a follower of Christ, have tried to live every day of your life. Jesus lives in you. He is present to your needs. He is your strength and your joy. He said, "Fear is useless; what you need is trust."

Taking Him at His word is something we all try to do. It's our mission in life to live this mystery. St. Paul put it simply, "I live – no – not I, but Christ lives in me."

The Catechism of the Catholic Church attempts to explain this mystery in paragraph 795 with a quote from St. Augustine, "Let us rejoice then, and give thanks that we have not only become Christians, but Christ himself. Do you understand and grasp this, my brethren? Marvel and rejoice, for you have become Christ. He is the head and you are the Body, together you make up the whole man."

Down through the centuries, Christians have maintained their dignity and carried out their mission in the face of trials, hardships and persecutions. Their deep faith has sustained them, and led them out of the darkness.

The Lord often stepped in to do for you what you could not do for yourself. Life is marvelously improved because of the Divine Presence within us. Through His Presence, Jesus gives us the wisdom that makes hope possible. The virtue of hope is defined as an expectation with certitude.

God loves you. You have the right to expect the best from your heavenly Father. You may not always be squeaky clean—none of us are—but you belong to Him. You are His child.

God's love empowers you to stay calm in the storms of life. It is possible to focus on His Presence within you. His Presence will empower you to bring peace, hope, and joy to your children and to all those whom you love. And it all begins by staying calm when you feel like running away.

"Then, if you spend yourself in behalf of others... then your light will rise in the darkness, and your night will become like the noonday." (Isaiah 58:10)

TELL A LOVED ONE YOU CARE

By Fr. John T. Catoir, JCD | August 31, 2009

The happiest moment of my life was the day of my ordination, May 28, 1960. My dear mother had died three years earlier, but, thankfully, my dad was there to share the joy. As he came forward for my first priestly blessing I could see that he was weeping a bit; I know I was. The moment had come at last. After all those years of study and preparation, I was finally an ordained priest of Jesus Christ.

Another happy day for Fr. John, when he received an Honorary Doctorate from St. John's University, New York. His father John T. Catoir, Sr. (right) was present for this honor as well.

Afterward, we all went out for a meal to celebrate the joyous event. My dad was thrilled to be the host of the party. I'm sure he said some touching things to me. It wasn't until 25 years later, however, that he wrote me a note to share his feelings about that day.

> "Dear Son, Congratulations on your Silver Jubilee. I never told you this before, but the fondest and happiest moment of my life was the day you were ordained and I went up to get your first blessing. I was so emotionally charged that as I returned up the aisle, I couldn't see where I was going. I just dropped into a vacant pew, buried my head, and had a good cry. They were happy tears, even though my one regret was that mother did not live long enough to share this joy with us. But I'm sure she enjoyed watching over us from heaven. Keep up the good work and pray for me always. I am happy to say that I am your father. With a heart full of love, Dad."

My eyes become a little teary when I read that note. Of all the honors and awards I've received in life, nothing compares with that communication from my father. It recaptured a special memory that I will always treasure. My dad died in 1992 at the age of 85.

Never underestimate the impact that a simple note to a loved one can have on them. Any attempt to express your deepest feelings will carry a lot of weight.

Why not think of someone you can share some noble thought with today. Someone dear to you will be especially grateful. A loving note might be just the thing they need right now to help them through a difficult time. Give someone the boost that only you can give.

TELL IT LIKE IT IS

By Fr. John T. Catoir, JCD | October 7, 2017

To some, the devil is nothing more than a silly Halloween costume. Nothing could be further from the truth.

The Las Vegas massacre cannot be explained as a mental health issue. It was pure evil that manifested itself as demonic madness. Those who deny the existence of Satanic malice have a lot to learn.

The Vatican has for centuries maintained archival records of diabolical possessions. A special school exists in the Holy See to train priests to be exorcists. To regard demonic behavior merely as a person's disconnection from reality is spiritual blindness.

Those who deny the existence of the devil need to realize that if you cut out all the sections of the Bible that mention the activity of Satan and the forces of darkness, the book would be left in shreds.

"The serpent is a liar, more crafty than any of the wild animals." God said, "You must not eat fruit from this tree or you will die." Later, Satan said, "You will certainly not die." (Genesis 3:1-5)

"But I am afraid that just as Eve was deceived by the serpent's cunning, your minds may somehow be led astray from your sincere and pure devotion to Christ." (2 Corinthians 11:3)

"The reason the Son of God appeared was to destroy the devil's work." (1 John 3:8) And, "I came that your joy may be full." (John 15:11)

Before the local leaders picked up stones to throw at Jesus, He said to them, "You belong to the devil; he is your father, and you want to carry out your father's desires. He was a murderer from the beginning, not holding to the truth. When Satan lies, he speaks his native tongue for he is a liar and the father of lies...then Jesus hid himself and went out of the temple." (John 8:44, 59)

"Submit yourself to God. Resist the devil, and he will flee from you." (James 4:7)

"Be alert and of sober mind. Your enemy the devil prowls around like a roaring lion looking for someone to devour. Resist him, standing in the faith." (1 Peter 5:8)

Then Peter said, "Ananias, how is it that Satan has so filled your heart that you have kept for yourself some of the money you received for the land?" (Acts 5:3)

"Put on the full armor of God, so that you can take your stand against the devil's schemes. For our struggle is not against flesh and blood, but against the powers of darkness, and against the spiritual forces of evil in the heavenly realms." (Ephesians 6:11-16)

Jesus said, "Fear is useless; what you need is trust." (Luke 8:50)

It is because I care that I present these truths to you. A good father wants to protect his children from all danger, visible and invisible. Yes, it's scary, it's upsetting, I know; but it is the truth.

I worry about all the high school kids who were taught by their science teacher never to believe anything you can't prove scientifically. To that I say, just look at the slaughter that took place in Las Vegas. There is evidence from all over the world where Muslim Jihadist terrorists have mercilessly massacred thousands, even while they are at worship. Is that evidence enough for you? Tell it like it is.

May the Lord be your strength and your joy.

THE AFTERLIFE
By Fr. John T. Catoir, JCD | February 5, 2018

Jesus taught us to say, "Our Father, who art in heaven." Our faith is based on the realization that there is an afterlife.

The next life has been part of our thinking since we were little children. But in this new age of science, it has become fashionable to withhold belief in anything that cannot be proven scientifically. Let me tell you straight up: that statement is a formula for disaster.

Unless you have a personal relationship with the inner life of God, which comes through Christ Our Lord, you cannot enter the Kingdom of Heaven. We know this by faith.

These are the kinds of things that science teaches: the distance of planet earth to the moon, the speed of light, and a whole warehouse of useless information, in terms of eternity. Science is of no help. No, let me correct that, science has taught us some lovely things. For instance, we know through science that the Neanderthal man loved flowers and that he buried the dead with tools to help them on their journey in the next life.

Aha! Belief in an afterlife came early. This supports the truth that belief in the hereafter is virtually universal. C.S. Lewis stressed the fact that, "The Church will outlive the universe." He continued, "We know from science that the time will come when every culture and every nation in the world will disappear. In fact, the entire human race and every biological form of life on planet earth will become extinct."

This raises the existential question, where will you be when everything else has disappeared? Science says, "Not a problem, you won't exist anymore, so it won't matter! But they can't prove that scientifically. How can they be so sure of what they can't prove?

The fact is that legions upon legions of human beings have known through intuition that life extends beyond this world.

We seldom see the hidden hand of God at work in this world, but we know by faith that God is always active in human history. We know that God has called us to be with Him forever in Heaven. We may not know exactly what life will be like in the next world, but we do know that God has a plan. Namely, He wants to share His eternal life with us.

The Catholic Catechism states that the Mystical Body of Christ includes everyone whom God claims as His own, even those outside the Church, and even those who lived before Christ was born. Our faith teaches us that God's mercy is infinite, and that all the good people of old who desired to do God's will throughout their lifetime, are part of the Kingdom of Heaven.

His mercy endures forever. The mystery of Divine Mercy is rejected by the world of science. "Therein lies the maddening ambiguity of our faith as it appears to others," said, C.S. Lewis, "As private individuals, as mere biological entities, we humans may appear to be of little account, but as an organic part of the Body of Christ, we are assured that we shall live to remember the galaxies as an old tale."

Jesus Christ said, 'In my house, there are many mansions...peace be with you."

May the Lord be your strength and your joy as you journey from this world to the next.

THE BATTLE AGAINST PEDOPHILIA
By Fr. John T. Catoir, JCD | August 20, 2018

For centuries, the clergy of all faiths have attracted deviants and con-artists who need the cloak of respectability to win the trust of their victims. We must do a better job of weeding them out. The outrage over the pedophile sexual abuse scandal in Pennsylvania is not strong enough; these crimes are beyond horrific. Support for the betrayed victims is our priority. Everyone is ashamed and devastated by this scandal, especially the good priests who detest these crimes and are often painted with the same brush. This terrible evil which has stained the face of Christ must be eliminated.

In the past, the Bishops dealt with sex abuse cases the way they dealt with alcohol abuse: repentance, forgiveness, rehabilitation, and recovery. Then, after a period of rehabilitation, a psychiatrist would write a letter to the effect that the priest was ready to return to active duty. Bishops thought this policy of mercy would work as it did with alcoholic priests. They were wrong. It failed miserably with pedophiles and is no longer considered valid. Today, many bishops are immediately turning sex-abuse accusations over to the police and letting law enforcement authorities determine if the charges are credible. If the priest is found guilty, he is sent to jail. Some of them have committed suicide, many have resigned from the priesthood knowing their career is over anyway.

The Pennsylvania Grand Jury deliberated over cases going back 70 years and found 300 guilty priests. During that period, there were about 30,000 priests who lived and died in the six Dioceses of Pennsylvania during that period: Philadelphia, Pittsburgh, Greensburg, Altoona, Erie and Harrisburg. Three hundred priests represent one percent of the total.

Bishop Donald Trautman, the Bishop of Erie, Pennsylvania from 1990 until his 2012 retirement at age 76, wondered if the Grand Jury told the whole story. He said, "I neither condoned nor enabled clergy abuse. Rather, I did just the opposite. My time spent as Bishop of the Diocese addressing sexual abuse has been the most demoralizing, trying, and pain-filled experience of my life. I have seen first hand how the terrible acts of the clergy abusers devastate the lives of innocent victims."

He commended the Grand Jury saying, "They rightfully chastised clergy who committed horrible crimes against children, but unfortunately, did not emphasize the concrete steps Church leaders took to correct and curtail abuse and help victims." The Bishop said that his record includes disciplining, defrocking and, ultimately, laicizing pedophile priests. "It also includes efforts to provide care and support for victims," which statement he supported by appending many letters from victims expressing gratitude for his pastoral care. I know Bishop Trautman to be a straight-shooter, and a champion of the laity. He's one of many bishops who is reversing the failed policies of the past.

The battle must go on. Let's also pray for everyone concerned: the victims and their parents, the priests – both innocent and guilty – and all those who have left the Church because of this scandal.

May the Lord continue to be their strength and their joy.

THE BIRTH OF JESUS CHRIST
By Fr. John T. Catoir, JCD | February 22, 2019

Over the years, many readers have asked me to repeat a column I wrote a few years ago. The article contained an excerpt written by Anna Katharina Emmerich, a mystic born of devout parents in Westphalia, Germany in 1774.

At 28 she entered the Augustinian convent a few miles away from her home. A few years later, in 1811, Napoleon Bonaparte was on the rampage suppressing all religious communities and all the nuns were forced to flee from their convents.

Katharina was given shelter by a kind family and remained with them until her death in 1824. A few months after her arrival, she received the stigmata. The wounds of the Passion of Christ appeared on her hands, feet, and side. Soon she began receiving mystical revelations about the life of Jesus. Scripture scholars have been amazed at the accuracy of her knowledge concerning the geography, language, and culture of the times in which Jesus lived and died.

Filmmaker Mel Gibson used her revelations as the basis of his movie, *The Passion of the Christ*. The following passage is about the birth of Jesus:

"Mary begged Joseph to do all in his power to find a fitting place for the birth of Jesus. This Child, promised by God, was supernaturally conceived. She invited Joseph to unite with her in prayer for the hard-hearted people who earlier refused them shelter. Joseph proposed bringing some pious women whom he knew in Bethlehem to her assistance; but Mary would not allow it. She declared that she had no need of anyone.

"It was five o'clock in the evening when Joseph brought Mary to a cave, one that he knew from childhood and which served as a shelter for shepherds in bad weather. He hung up several lamps and made a place for their animal.

"When Mary told Joseph that her time was drawing near and that he should now betake himself to prayer, he did her bidding and left her, turning toward his sleeping place. Before entering his little recess, he looked back once toward that part of the cave where Mary knelt in prayer, her back to him. He saw the cave filled with a light that streamed from Mary. It was as if he were like Moses, looking into the burning bush. He sank prostrate to the ground in prayer and looked not back again. The glory around Mary became brighter and brighter, and the lamps that Joseph had lit were no longer to be seen. Mary knelt, her flowing robe spread out before her. At the twelfth hour, her prayer became ecstatic…the light around her grew even more resplendent. At that moment, she gave birth to the infant Jesus. I saw Him, a tiny child far brighter than all the other brilliancy.

"Mary's ecstasy lasted some moments longer. Then I saw her spread a cover over the Child, but she did not yet take Him up. I saw the Child stirring and heard it crying, and only then did Mary seem to recover full consciousness. She lifted the Child to her breast and sat veiled. I saw angels around her in human form prostrate on their faces…

"Sometime after the birth, Mary called Joseph who was still prostrate in prayer, and urged him to look upon the Sacred Gift from Heaven, and then Joseph came and took the Child into his arms."

THE BOTTOM LINE

By Fr. John T. Catoir, JCD | December 1, 2017

What are you looking to accomplish with your life? For you, what is the bottom line of your existence? The Catholic perspective on this question is that the supreme purpose of every human being is to save his or her soul. We do this by accepting Jesus as Lord, and by helping others to save their souls.

Becoming a holy Christian takes time, so be patient with yourself. If you think you may need a little more maturing, you're probably right. I'm 86 and I'm just beginning to get the hang of it. One either keeps on maturing or one falls by the wayside. I'm never surprised when people slip in the practice of their faith.

However, if the lapse causes them to forget their primary purpose, namely, saving their immortal soul, it sets off an alarm in my head. I recall how St. Paul was exceedingly upset when he found out that many of his Roman converts were falling back into paganism. He reasoned that it's one thing to lapse into neglect, but quite another to lose your faith entirely. He wrote to them to shape them up.

Losing one's faith happens slowly over an extended period; it's hardly noticeable. Here's a check list to help you see how you're doing. Ask yourself the following questions:

Am I a good Catholic or merely a pagan with Catholic patches? Do I truly love Jesus Christ? Do I believe He is truly present in the Eucharist? Do I go to Mass on Sundays and receive Holy Communion? Do I read the Word of God often, seldom, or never?

We're all sinners and we all need to check our progress from time to time. One sure sign of a true believer is that he or she prays. Prayer consists of Adoration, Repentance, Thanksgiving, and Petition. How are you doing in the prayer department?

It pleases the Lord when we pray for ourselves and others. He wants to be your best friend. From time to time, pray for the whole Church. Pray for those who stumble and fall. Pray for the spirit of forgiveness. Pray for the ability to trust the Lord. Pray for the joy of the Holy Spirit. Pray for the virtues of faith, hope, and charity, and pray to be open to God's grace.

Openness means placing yourself in the hands of God and trusting His love. Surprisingly, your holiness depends more on God's love for you than it does on your love for God. Nevertheless, you must try to make a reasonable effort to be holy.

So many people are afraid and lonely. They compound their problem by falling away from the community of Faith. This is sad because it's so much more difficult to "seek first the Kingdom of God" when you try to do it on your own. You can show your love for the Lord by caring for those in need, especially if they are all alone.

God has asked us to offer Him public worship. Jesus said, "Do this in memory of Me." A good Catholic attends Holy Mass on Sunday not only because it is a form of obedience to His will, but because it advances the very purpose of their life. They want to be faithful to the bottom line, and win eternal happiness in heaven.

May the Lord be your strength and your joy.

THE CROSS AND JOY

By Fr. John T. Catoir, JCD | March 8, 2009

God wants you to be happy, even though life is filled with misery. There will always be crosses and yet, we are called to live joyfully.

St. Paul helps us to master the Christian faith by understanding the relationship between God's love for us and the trials we have to endure in this world.

We all suffer physical and emotional pain of some sort: our bodies ache, people disappoint and abuse us, financial woes engender fear in us, and yet we are still called to live joyfully. St. Paul, who suffered mightily in his day, commanded us to, "Rejoice always!"

I write about joy all the time and I suppose I get on the nerves of some people. However, I feel driven by the Holy Spirit. Occasionally, St. Paul felt driven to boast about his many trials for the glory of God and I feel that need right now.

In my Army days, I fired an M1 rifle for endless hours on a practice range. I was an MP and the company commander wanted us to fire 'expert.' This bombardment of noise left me with a fierce buzzing in my ears to this day. I cope by uniting my inner buzzing with the song the angels sing before the Lord. My tinnitus is no longer my enemy, but has become my friend, enabling me to pray with out ceasing.

I have ulcerative colitis and my 77 year-old arthritic knees give me fits. I'm a cancer survivor, so far that is, and I suffer from cardiac asthma. And, yet, I get through it all by following St. Paul's advice to "thank God in all circumstances." His advice has kept me sane. All of my little miseries are under control with medication. I love my life and my vocation. I love to write, which is a vocation within a vocation, and I especially enjoy maintaining my web site: www. messengerofjoy.com *(Ed. Note: now www.johncatoir)*, which offers tips for being more joyful to anyone who asks.

How do we know that God loves us? It's simple really. Jesus Christ told us to call God "Our Father." Doesn't every father want his children to be happy? That's why St. Paul said, "Rejoice always, and be grateful in all circumstances, for this is the will of God for you in Christ Jesus." (I Corinthians 5:16) He took this magnificent idea from Jesus who, at the last supper said, "I have told you all these things that my joy may be in you, and your joy may be complete." (John 15:11)

Pope John Paul II confirmed it: "Christ came to bring joy. Joy to children, joy to parents, joy to families and friends, joy to workers and scholars, joy to the sick and elderly, joy to all humanity. In a true sense, joy is the keynote message and the recurring motif of the Gospels. Go therefore and become messengers of joy." Our response ought to be, "Yes, I will be glad and filled with joy, because of You." (Psalm 9:2)

What about the cross?

When Jesus told us to, "Love one another as I have loved you," he led us to the cross. Wherever there is love there is service, wherever there is service there is sacrifice, and wherever there is sacrifice there is the cross. Joy and the cross are not contradictory, but complimentary. Jesus knew that the only way to find true joy was to empty oneself in loving others.

"The greatest honor you can give to Almighty God is to live joyfully because of the knowledge of his love." – Julian of Norwich

THE FALLEN HUMAN RACE

By Fr. John T. Catoir, JCD | October 27, 2018

Beware all you Catholics who left your religion behind because of your misguided acceptance of Darwin's atheistic theory of evolution. Albert Einstein was correct when he said, "There must be a supreme intelligence behind the universe." The Book of Genesis is not literal history. However, it is Divine Revelation. The Adam and Eve story is a parable that teaches us the Divinely inspired truth that we are living in a fallen state.

The doctrine of Original Sin proclaims the fallen state of mankind. Original Sin makes us morally weak and causes many to despise the truth. Our weakened human nature is especially evident in our widespread acts of war. In the 19th century, the carnage of many wars devastated the world and destroyed millions of lives. How does Darwin's theory of evolution tie into this?

Look at the Nazis and the Marxist Communists. Both groups are grounded in the concept of "The Super Race," which came right out of Darwin's theory. The Nazis believed they had the right to purify the super race by killing Jews, Gypsies, Negroes and, yes, even Catholics, all of whom were the targets of their mass murders. The Jews were the most hated; 6 million of them were cruelly murdered.

The doctrine of original sin is the result of Adam's refusal to obey the will of God. Today's world is on the brink of exploding once again for the same reason. Hatred still prevails over love. We fail to seek first the Kingdom of God.

The Atheistic Evolution Theory of Darwin's is disputed even within his own inner circle. They divide in two main camps: 1) the Gradualists and 2) the Saltationists. The first group of Gradualists maintain that human beings have evolved gradually over the centuries through minor changes and major leaps of one species into another up until the final stage, when the apes turned into men, through a process Darwin called "natural selection."

The Saltationists strongly disagreed, saying there is NO SCIENTIFIC evidence to prove Darwin's theory of gradualism. The Saltationists offered their own strange and unscientific explanation. They said that new species do appear, but only suddenly, after millions of years of stability; that a reptile one day laid an egg which produced a bird. Centuries later, the birds produced eggs which carried a baby mammal. Both groups do agree on one point; namely, that evolution itself came about without any Divine intervention.

"If any sane person believes this stuff, then he surely must believe in fairy tales," says Larry Azar, author of a 619-page book, with 42 pages of bibliography, entitled, *Evolution and Other Fairy Tales*. It is an examination of the logic and cogency of Darwin's arguments, and concludes stating that there is no evidence given whatsoever to prove Darwin's Theory of Atheistic Evolution.

Science openly admits that it cannot explain the origins of the human race. Popes John Paul II, Benedict XVI, and Pope Francis have all approved the concept of "Theistic Evolution", which states that God is the first cause of everything in the created universe and admits that changes have evolved within each species due to growth and adaptation.

Peace be with you. May the Lord be your strength.

THE FIRST AMENDMENT AND YOU
By Fr. John T. Catoir, JCD | October 10, 2017

Obamacare violated the religious rights of the Little Sisters of the Poor, Texas Baptist University and five other litigants who challenged its mandate to pay for and distribute contraceptives under the penalty of a fine. On Nov. 6, 2015, the Supreme Court blocked the Obamacare contraceptive mandate from being enforced. Congress later admitted the government was wrong to impose it and apologized to the litigants.

To understand the legality of the issue better, a brief review of Constitutional law is necessary. The First Amendment of the U.S. Constitution is a rule of law designed to protect the rights of individual citizens. Their freedom to follow their religious convictions was only one of the rights guaranteed by the First Amendment:

"Congress shall make no law respecting an establishment of religion, or prohibiting the free exercise thereof; or abridging the freedom of speech; or of the press; or the right of the people peaceably to assemble, and to petition the Government for a redress of grievances."

The Preamble to the U.S. Constitution states its purpose: "to establish justice, insure domestic tranquility, provide for the common defense, promote the general welfare, and secure the blessings of liberty to ourselves and our posterity."

After the Preamble, there are Seven articles in the Constitution, each with many sections. The Seventh and final article was passed unanimously on Sept. 17th, 1787, and signed by George Washington, the assembly President, and by all the representatives. Four years later, on Sept. 25, 1791, the First Amendment to the Constitution was approved.

The First Amendment Right to petition the Government for a redress of grievances was duly exercised by the Little Sisters of the Poor, et al. Later, President Trump extended this right beyond religious bodies and non-profit organizations to include all American citizens. The central issue was never about the use of contraceptives. It was always about the legality of any mandate forcing citizens, under the penalty of a fine, to pay for and distribute contraceptives.

It should be noted that many Catholics use contraceptives in good conscience. In moral matters, when doubts arise in matters of conscience, a Catholic has the right and the duty to follow his or her conscience. The Church teaches that conscience does not replace the Church's Magisterium, it merely applies the teaching of the Church to individual circumstances.

On the issue of birth control, the late moral theologian Father Bernard Haring put it this way: "Whoever is convinced that the absolute forbidding of artificial means of birth control is the correct interpretation of divine law, must earnestly endeavor to live according to this conviction. However, anyone who after serious reflection and prayer, is convinced that in his or her case such a prohibition could NOT be the will of God, should in peace follow his/her conscience, and not thereby feel like a second-class Catholic."

All American citizens are free to follow their consciences on the use of contraceptives. They just can't require other Americans who are opposed to the practice to pay for their contraceptives.

Why doesn't the same principle apply to the government's use of taxpayer's money to pay for abortions? Government funding of abortion mills like Planned Parenthood violates the conscience of many Americans. Citizens of all faiths are forced to finance a practice they find morally abhorrent. Why is this allowed?

THE HIDDEN HAND OF GOD

By Fr. John T. Catoir, JCD | September 21, 2017

Congratulations to Editor Richard Sokerka and his great staff for the splendid 80th anniversary issue of *The Beacon*, the newspaper of the Diocese of Paterson, New Jersey. It made me think of the hidden hand of God behind all those statistics and events.

Our Diocese has grown in wisdom, age and grace since its inception in 1937. It would take volumes to tell the whole story, but even then, the mystery of God's role in all of it would be hidden from or eyes. God bless you all for your cooperation in God's plan of salvation.

What we see before us is a community of faith that has grown in bits and pieces, by God's grace, with the help of thousands of men and women. Behind all the events of our history, the Lord was always there supplying us with His strength and His joy.

We only scratch the surface when we read about the many parish openings, school graduations, Mass celebrations, episcopal visitations, first communions, weddings, ordinations and the like. We want to give God the glory for all that He has done for us over the years.

Faith is the knowledge that comes to us from Divine Revelation. There is One Faith, One People, and One Lord, Jesus Christ. We believe in the invisible interaction that has taken place between God and His faithful people over these 80 years because the Church believes in the perfectibility of man.

We aspire to holiness. The transformation of a human soul from mediocrity to sainthood is a pure mystery. The Lord infuses us with His grace through the sacraments: Baptism, Holy Communion, Confirmation, Matrimony, Penance, the Sacrament of the Sick, and Ordination. Each sacrament is an outward sign instituted by God to give grace.

One of the great accomplishments of the Church under God's guidance has been the creation of our Catholic school system. Parents believe that it is necessary to give children a solid spiritual foundation from the first grade to college. We want to prepare them with the fortitude that comes from a strong faith.

There is a drug sub-culture out there that is seducing kids and young adults by the millions. They need all the spiritual help they can get. The hidden hand of God has inspired the sisters, priests, brothers, and lay teachers to serve our children. These men and woman have answered an inner calling from God.

The sisters and teachers instruct the children with skill and devotion. The priests provide services ranging from administration to offering Masses to teaching and counseling. Our good lay teachers have made financial sacrifices to use their talents serving our Catholic School children. All this is being done for the glory to God.

Every parish strives to offer their parishioners a welcoming environment, a place to experience Christ—not only in one another, but in the Eucharist. Jesus is truly present in every tabernacle from Sussex to Morristown to Passaic and throughout the world.

Over the years, our bishops have been strengthened by God's grace to establish, organize, and manage a network of 111 parishes. Together we have grown into a community of love. Under God's protection and guidance, we have prospered – thanks be to God.

Happy Anniversary, and may the Lord continue to be your strength and your joy.

THE JOYFUL SEASON OF LENT

By Fr. John T. Catoir, JCD | March 6, 2019

There is a famous quote from St. John Chrysostom that draws attention to the supreme purpose of Lent; namely, the celebration of Easter. "Every year we celebrate Easter, the greatest and most shining feast of the Liturgical calendar."

From the beginning, the Lenten Liturgy has been filled with references to joy, not only because it is a time of preparation for the coming Feast of the Resurrection of Jesus, but also because our purification through prayer and fasting brings a special form of delight to the soul.

We need to think of Lent as both a time of joy and a time of penance. This is not a new idea. Gregory the Great, who was pope at the turn of the sixth century A.D., emphasized the theme of joy. He spoke of the two-fold path before us: the way of life that leads to joy, and the way of death that leads to misery and damnation. He quoted from the first Psalm to make his point: "Happy the man who follows not the counsel of the wicked."

Lent is a forty-day period devoted to prayer, fasting, and almsgiving. It is designed to help us focus on the mystery of our redemption. Through it all, we are all called to live joyfully because of the knowledge of God's love. Yes, we must fast because there is always a need for penance.

Think of Lent as part of a musical prelude to the joyful symphony of Easter. The entire celebration lasts fifty days beyond Easter Sunday, right up to Pentecost Sunday, the birthday of the Church. During this Easter cycle, we anticipate the celebration, the gift of the Holy Spirit coming down upon the Church. The ultimate feast of celebration comes when Jesus returns to us at the end of time.

But fasting helps us to free ourselves from the things of this world. Things that can diminish our desire to put first things first; namely the love of God, the love of neighbor and love of self. Fasting is particularly helpful for those who are addicted in some way—to drugs or some other vice. Think about it. Greed is an acquisitive spirit; anger is often a lust for vengeance. Jealousy is the constant fear that someone is taking what is rightly yours. Envy is sadness over the good fortune of another, and lust is an inordinate attraction to sex.

Almsgiving helps us to cultivating a generous spirit. We pray for the strength to put God above all things. Abbot John Chapman, an English Benedictine, wisely said, "The only way to pray well is to pray often. Pure prayer is in the will to give yourself to God. You never have to force feelings of any kind."

Jesus is our role model and exemplar. He prayed and fasted for forty days in the desert before he began his public ministry. During Lent we try to imitate him. "I have set you an example, that you also should do as I do." (John 13:15)

Love is the supreme law and the ultimate purpose of our Lenten discipline. In loving us, Jesus entered His public ministry and faced hardship and rejection. He was scorned, humiliated, and betrayed by one of his own. And yet he carried on, leaving us a legacy of perseverance, hope, and joy.

"In this world you will have many troubles, but cheer up and take heart, for I have overcome the world." (John 16:33)

THE JOY OF FORGIVENESS

By Fr. John T. Catoir, JCD | October 1, 2017

The poet Yeats once alluded to a special moment of joy in his life, a time when he experienced an unexpected elation. "My body, all of a sudden, blazed." He had forgiven someone and was free once again to dance in the presence of his loving God. Meister Eckhart, the German mystic wrote, "For this Joy is close to you; it is in you. None of you has a spirit so heavy, nor an intelligence so feeble, nor are any of you so far from God so as not to be able to find this Joy in Him."

Normally, one does not feel like forgiving. Anger and resentment block the desire for reconciliation. But when you invite the Spirit of the Lord in, and allow Him to abide within you, you will find the strength to forgive. Then a real relief follows, either suddenly as in the case of Yeats, or gradually over time.

To attain the spirit of pure forgiveness, you need to pray for it. Forgiveness comes from God. When Jesus said, "Forgive them Father, for they know not what they do" (Luke 23:34), He forgave His tormentors before they even asked. He forgave them without any conditions.

There are two things that are important to remember if you want to attain pure forgiveness: it is unconditional and not based on feelings.

1. Pure forgiveness is in the will, and the will says 'yes' or 'no'! There are no ifs, ands, or buts. You don't say, "I'm ready to forgive, but you must first do the following before I give you my final 'yes'." Pure forgiveness is unconditional.

2. Do not wait for warm feelings of forgiveness to kick in; they may never come. You forgive because Jesus asks you to forgive, not because the person deserves it or asks for it. You forgive before you feel comfortable doing it. You give it before you feel like it. And you do not force feelings of any kind. It's not hypocritical to feel resentment while you say, "Yes, I forgive you."

The feelings of hurt and resentment may not dissolve right away, but there is usually a sense of relief that comes soon. In the case of the poet Yeats, it was a real high, but the average person may continue to feel anger welling up from time to time. Forgiveness turns off the furnace, but the building needs time to cool down. Learn to laugh at your anger. Just know that you are clean, in harmony with God's will, and pleasing to Jesus because you obediently followed His good example.

Pope St. John Paul II explained how the process works when you receive the forgiveness yourself. "The repentant sinner is reconciled with himself in his inmost being where he regains his identity. He is reconciled with his brethren whom he has in some way attacked and wounded. He is reconciled with the victim of his crime, with the Church, and with all creation." But it is important to remember, Pope John Paul II did not try to get his would-be assassin released from jail. The justice issue is separate and must be respected. Criminals owe a debt to society.

THE JOY OF JESUS

By Fr. John T. Catoir, JCD | January 20, 2019

The Joy of Jesus is a Divine mystery, but Joy itself is something everyone understands. The Holy Spirit of Joy is a supernatural reality that comes to us in ordinary ways. At the tabernacle of every Catholic Church, we come together as one People forming the Mystical Body of Christ. We realize that we live in union with Jesus, "In Him we live and breathe and have our being." (Acts 17:28)

The Catholic Church is the oldest pan-national organization in the world. Empires have come and gone, but the Church has survived the storms and trials of life. The reason it is still standing, despite so many abuses and scandal, is because Jesus Christ, its founder, is both true God and true man. The Divine Love of Christ empowers Him to perform His saving mission. "I did not come to condemn, but to save the world." (John 3:17) Jesus returns good for evil in the form of joy, forgiveness, and healing. His love is infinite and universal.

Miraculously, the Church survives generation after generation despite the many sins of His people. Renewing itself repeatedly, the Church reveals a Divine Center rooted in God's love. In my book, *Joy, The Spirit's Gigantic Secret Behind the Church's Survival,* (Alba House, N.Y., 2006), I explore the miracle of the Church's miraculous self-purification. G.K. Chesterton said, "Joy is the gigantic secret of Christianity." Christ's Love is the deciding factor in our survival. His Love and Joy are two sides of the same coin.

Examine the words of Jesus and see how joy, love, and forgiveness have played such a vital role in the Church's salvific mission. The ability to achieve renewal year after year is an astounding miracle. The Sacrament of confession is a basic part of this ongoing miracle in the lives of saints and sinners.

Pope John Paul II took repentance to an entirely new level when He asked God to forgive all the sins the Church has committed over the centuries. Because the Church is made up of weak human beings, Pope John Paul II at the Second Vatican Council decided to name the Church "The Sinful People of God." He deplored and repented the many sexual scandals that have plagued the Church, especially those involving the sexual abuses committed by priests, bishops, and cardinals. He begged for forgiveness for the Church's mistreatment of Jews in past centuries, and repented the Church's abusive treatment of heretics in the Spanish Inquisition. He also repented of forty other distinct crimes that have offended God and shamed the Church.

Nevertheless, billions of people down through the ages have found Joy and solace in the Church, precisely because it has become for them a port in the storm of life. They have experienced great mercy from popes, bishops and priests in their routine sacramental ministry. Mercy increases and multiplies. Even many survivors of the sex-abuse scandals still love the Church.

The Doctrine of Original Sin traces man's sinfulness to Adam and Eve and their refusal to obey the will of God. The failure of humans to seek first the Kingdom of God has been a constant thorn in the side of Jesus. But His infinite Mercy has prevailed over sorrow. We are constantly blessed by Almighty God and His infinite mercy.

The sin of Adam and Eve is often referred to as, "O Felix culpa," Latin for "O happy fault, which brought about our salvation."

THE MARRIAGE TRIBUNAL

By Fr. John T. Catoir, JCD | October 22, 2018

Every Diocese in the Catholic Church has a judicial branch to handle legal matters involving marriage and divorce. The Church regards the bond of marriage between a man and a woman to be binding for life. However human nature being what it is, the best laid plans of brides and grooms often go astray. Among the marriages that fall apart, some are based on an invalid consent, which goes to the heart of the contract and makes the marriage invalid.

For example, you're not permitted to say, "I reserve the right to cheat any time I want." The Church has rules and won't marry you if you deviate from the terms of a valid contract, which requires a commitment to a permanence and exclusive union. If you secretly intend to be unfaithful to your spouse, you are giving a false consent that is ipso facto invalid. Such a marriage can be annulled.

In my many years as head of the Paterson Diocesan Tribunal, I concluded that the Tribunal system was making too many mistakes. Many courts are understaffed, and many canon lawyers lack sufficient training in the field of psychology. An annulment based on a defective consent is not easy to discern without a confession. Judges need a lot of wisdom and common sense. They do not always agree. A judge with a letter-of-the law mentality often renders an incorrect decision. Judicial wisdom sees more clearly than mathematical logic.

The grounds for nullity include the following: she was under legal age, he was once married and never told anyone, she lied when she said she intended a life-long union, he lied when he committed to an exclusive union, she lied when she said she was open to having children. Perhaps most common grounds being pleaded in recent years is psychic incapacity, when one or both parties lack the ability to enter and sustain the burdens and obligations of marriage.

In 1967, I wrote an article in *Commonwealth Magazine* entitled, *The Church and Second Marriage*. I challenged the wisdom of those who were rigidly obstructing justice. A month after my article appeared, the Canon Law Society of America elected me to their Board of Governors. Some cases were going on and on for more than ten years. Justice delayed is justice denied. I encouraged the laity to exercise their God-given right to freedom of conscience, if necessary.

Of course, there was some backlash. I was accused of being in favor of adultery. A few bishops called my bishop, urging him to fire me. Bishop Casey stood by me and kept me on as his Judicial Vicar. Eventually, the priests of my Diocese elected me to be their first full-time Clergy Personnel Director, and I breathed a sigh of relief.

If you have ever wondered why I am such a huge fan of Pope Francis, now you know. It was music to my ears when, in February of 2016, he encouraged the laity to place greater reliance on a "well-formed conscience". Those legalistic bishops who have unwisely challenged him may be well-intentioned but in my judgment, they are in error. I ask them: Is it better to send them the message that they're living in mortal sin when there is reasonable doubt about the truth of such a statement?

May the Lord be your strength and your Joy as you try to figure all this out.

THE OPTIMISM OF POPE JOHN XXIII

By Fr. John T. Catoir, JCD | May 7, 2017

Don't trust your pessimistic feelings. There was a great outpouring of elation from the laity and the clergy in 1959 when Pope John XXIII announced his plans to convene the Second Vatican Council. He was 68 years old and was considered too old to take on such a gigantic task. His optimism frightened the Cardinals who elected him.

They were shocked at his determination. He was considered an interim Pope. Instead of hoping for the best, many feared the worst. But Pope John knew that the Holy Spirit was guiding him, and he trusted Divine Providence with all his heart.

Pope John died in 1963 and was canonized in 2014, but the "Age of the Laity" which he unleashed had been slowly unfolding since 1965, the year that Vatican II concluded.

Many of the Cardinals who feared that he would go too far began opposing him. Pope John's response to all this was a public statement calling them "prophets of gloom and doom". He ignored his critics and went right on with his plans.

Today we find the same kind of pessimism. Many feel that the Church is slipping, and even going under. Nothing could be further from the truth. The facts tell a different tale. We are witnessing an on-going transformation in Christ that was initiated by Vatican II over 50 years ago, and it has shaken the Church to its roots.

Here are a few facts worth considering. There were 291 million Catholics in the world in 1910, today there are nearly 1.1 billion Catholics, according to Pew Research Centre. Wikipedia reports that there are now 70.4 million U.S. Catholics in communion with the Pope. That figure is up from approximately 50 million in 1970, and comprises 22% of the U.S. population.

Many parishes have closed or been consolidated to adjust to changing circumstances, but the number of converts and the influx of immigrants have kept our numbers on the rise. Also, fall-away Catholics have been returning in large numbers. A Gallup poll said that about 20% of lapsed Catholics are seriously thinking about returning to their roots.

As for the clergy shortage, we heard recently that Pope Francis is considering the ordination of married men of proven character to the priesthood. That may or may not happen, but the fact that the issue of celibacy is being thoughtfully reexamined is heartening. Remember that for 1,000 years, mandatory celibacy was not required for the priesthood.

The role of women in the Church is a matter of controversy, but all things considered, there have been some remarkable gains. We see many woman filling roles in the Church that were unthinkable 50 years ago. Some have been appointed as Diocesan Chancellors and many nuns have become parish administrators. This speaks, in a modest way, to the gradual declericalizaton of the Church.

Also, the laity today is much more involved in evangelization than ever before. Most Catholic missionary societies have added a dedicated support system of lay men and women devoting their lives to the foreign missions. And charitable donations are up considerably. This financial support forms the backbone of all our missionary efforts in helping Catholics and people of all faiths.

I leave you with this thought which is taken from mental health experts worldwide: feelings are not facts. The Church is Holy and very much alive, all negative feelings to the contrary.

THE PRIESTHOOD AND THE LAITY
By Fr. John T. Catoir, JCD | October 30, 2017

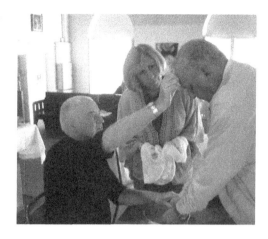

From time to time someone asks me, "What's it like to be a priest? What keeps you going? I wonder, did you ever have a similar question? If so, the answer is simple: the very same thing that keeps me going is what keeps you going; namely, my faith.

A priest's mission consists in living the mystery of the Presence of Jesus Christ. "I live, no not I, but Christ lives in me." I suspect the same is true for you because it's true for every member of the Mystical Body of Christ. This mystery is explained in the Catechism of the Catholic Church, paragraph 795, with quotes from St. Augustine and St. Joan of Arc.

St. Augustine wrote, "Let us rejoice and give thanks that we have become not only Christians, but Christ Himself". He goes on, "Do you understand this? You should marvel and rejoice for you have become Christ: He is the head and you are the members; together we all make up the whole man." Our souls are animated by the same Holy Spirit.

St. Joan of Arc said this to her judges before they condemned her to be burned at the stake, "I love the Church, I will always love the Church because for me, the Church is Jesus Christ." Keep in mind that the Church is defined as the People of God. This means that each one of us is a carrier of Christ. The Presence of Jesus abides in the souls of everyone who strives to be in the state of grace.

St. Joan concluded her recorded testimony with these words, "I simply know that Jesus Christ and the Church are one and the same thing." This uneducated teenager knew intuitively that the Church;

namely, the priests, bishops and the laity combined, make up one Mystical Body.

Granted, a priest is a specially chosen channel of communication with the Divine. Nevertheless, he is an ordinary person, a forgiven sinner, and a vessel of clay. He is human, as we all know, and he needs the strength of Jesus to keep on going.

My point is not to diminish the dignity of the priesthood, but to emphasize the dignity of the average lay person. The Presence of Christ is just as real in each of them. Membership in the Mystical Body of Christ confers on every member a special dignity. The gift of the Presence of Christ makes us all a new creation.

In a real sense, because of the Presence of Christ, laymen and women have an extraordinary vocation as well. As carriers of Christ, they can make a difference in this world, both as parents and as leaders. Marriage is an extraordinary vocation. Husbands and wives minister the Sacrament of Matrimony to one another, and bring new life into the world. As guardians of their children they influence the social order for the good.

The Church is the visible sign of the Presence of Christ. Each one of us, at any time, can call on Jesus in whom we live and breathe and have our being. We are thereby empowered to fulfill the duties and obligations of our state in life because we are most wonderfully blessed.

May the Lord be your strength and your joy.

THERE IS NOBODY LIKE YOU

By Fr. John T. Catoir, JCD | November 16, 2017

God is always acting in our lives, sometimes subtly and sometimes dramatically. I firmly believe that the future of the world will be more joyful because God is continually supplying us with the graces we need to help make this a better world.

Theologically, actual grace is defined as a light to your mind or an impulse to your will, coming directly from the mind of God. He influences us without taking away our freedom. He prods to take action. We may not understand the process as it's happening, but His graces are very effective.

Permit me to tell you a two-part story from my life where God intervened and changed my world. The first part of the story has to do with my vocational calling. I didn't want to be a priest, but I did aspire to be holy. I wanted marriage and a family, but somehow, I became more and more attracted to the priesthood. God eventually wore me down. I entered the seminary and was ordained in 1960. I never looked back.

The second part happened 17 years later. I learned that a Catholic multi-media organization called The Christophers needed a new director. Their founder, Father James Keller, had died. My father gave me Father Keller's book *You Can Change the World* on my eighteenth birthday, and I savored every word of it.

After working as a Catholic priest in various parishes for 17 years, and overseeing the Marriage Tribunal of the Diocese of Paterson for ten years, I felt the need for a new challenge. I knew that I didn't have the experience to run a media organization, so I concluded, "Why even bother to apply?"

Fears and apprehensions killed my initial enthusiasm and for three weeks I did nothing. Then, BINGO, a burst of energy hit me. I suddenly thought, "What have I got to lose?" I decided to write a letter to the Christopher Board of Directors realizing that the only thing holding me back was my fear of being rejected.

It took exactly one year and two interviews from the time I applied until the board called to tell me that they had chosen me to be their

new Director. I was flabbergasted, jubilant, and extremely grateful.

Looking back, I now see how the grace of God led me to the priesthood and later to become the successor to my boyhood idol, Father Keller. It's extremely important for all of us to see the connection between God's grace and the decisions we make in life. We should never allow fear to prevail over the noble desires of the heart.

For the next 18 years, I appeared on radio and television shows, wrote books and articles, and gave talks around the world; all aimed at bringing the Christopher message to a wider audience. "God has a job for you to do that nobody else can do. There is no one like you. You CAN make a difference."

In conclusion, I gladly repeat that message. We need what only you can give; first to the people around you and then to the world beyond. There's nobody like you, and with the help of God, you can make this a better world.

May the Lord be your strength and your joy.

THE THEOLOGY OF CHRISTMAS

By Fr. John T. Catoir, JCD | November 28, 2018

On the Feast of the Incarnation, we celebrate Almighty God's decision to become man by assuming the body of a human being. The Heavenly Father announced to Mary that she was chosen to be the Mother of God's only Begotten Son. Mary had been immaculately conceived in her mother's womb and was made ready from her conception for this supreme moment in the history of the world.

Mary humbly accepted the Divine invitation and submitted to the will of her Heavenly Father in all things. When her time came, she gave birth to an infant boy and named him Jesus. Being truly human, "He grew in wisdom, age and grace." This Divine Mystery is beyond our ability to comprehend fully but we are all privy to the facts that surround the Mystery.

It is important to know that the human and divine natures of Jesus are not mixed; one does not dissolve into the other. We accept this on faith. Jesus is one Divine Person with two natures. The human and divine natures in Jesus Christ coexist without becoming commingled. His humanity is always fully present. And yet, Jesus is one Divine Person, God incarnate.

Mary was just as perplexed as you are. She accepted her vocation in a state of wonder. She understood that the long-awaited Messiah was to be taken from her body. Jesus is flesh of her flesh and bone of her bone. The Lord was carried in her womb for nine months, and when her time came, God Incarnate was born in the form of a tiny infant.

The process by which Jesus became a Divine Person began in the Father's love. He wanted to become totally united to all of us and made it possible for us to become members of the Mystical Body of Christ. The reception of this gift is given either in the Sacrament of Baptism or in the Sacrament of Ardent Desire for union with The Lord. We become other Christs. "In Him we live, and breathe and have our being." God initiated this divinization process by allowing us to become one with the inner life of Jesus. At each reception of Holy

Communion, we become more and more transformed into Our Lord's Life. Our new status enables us to be Christ-bearers in our service to one another.

Jesus was born in Bethlehem, but was it in a stable or a cave? Some accept the mystical revelations of Katharina Emmerich; namely, that Jesus was born in a cave where shepherds came to give shelter to their sheep. St. Joseph, who knew the area from his boyhood, acted when he realized that there was no room at the inn. He brought Mary to that cave for shelter. They traveled to the outskirts of Bethlehem and settled in a cold, damp cave to prepare for the birth of Christ the King. The most important event in the history of the world, the Birth of Christ, which we refer to as the Feast of the Incarnation, took place in a cave where the body of Jesus was warmed by the breath of beasts.

On a personal note, the sentiments of my Christmas card are extended to one and all, "Wishing you the love Jesus, Mary and Joseph knew on that first Christmas night. May you and your loved ones share the peace and happiness of that love with each other."

THE WILL SAYS YES OR NO

By Fr. John T. Catoir, JCD | January 1, 2008

Jim wanted to quit smoking. Whenever the New Year came around, he felt discouraged. Having broken so many resolutions in the past, he was afraid of trying again. He just couldn't kick the habit.

It wasn't because he was weak. Jim would climb Mount Everest in a snowstorm to get a smoke if he needed to. What he lacked was a game plan. He needed to know more about the human psyche.

The soul is made up of intellect and will. The will is the center of the personality. The will says "Yes" or No." The will can only control the thoughts, the thoughts in turn control the feelings, and the emotions in turn control the actions.

The will says "yes" or "no" to your thoughts. It has no direct control over your actions. To get to your actions, the will has to go through the thoughts, which make the feelings change. Feelings and cravings can drive you to act against your own best intentions. Learn to condition your feelings by working hard to control your thoughts.

You are not your thoughts. You are the observer of your thoughts. Thoughts come and go willy-nilly; some are healthy and some are toxic. You are the center of your personality. You control your will to say "yes" to healthy thoughts and "no" to toxic ones. Toxic thoughts create toxic feelings. Here is a typical toxic thought: "I need a fix, no matter what!"

This is a false belief which will upset your emotions. You have to reject it with all your heart. Contradict your toxic thinking with positive thoughts. Decide to crave good health. Decide to be happy. Decide to become your own best friend. Decide to love yourself by believing that you are called by God to be an instrument of joy. Decide to rise to the highest aspirations of the human spirit. Smoking will damage your health, make you angry with yourself, and interfere with your vocation.

The more you think about being healthy, the less you will want to fill your lungs with poisonous smoke. Controlling your thoughts is at the very heart of all spiritual progress. Most people live by their feelings, but feelings are ultimately shaped by your thoughts. Control your thoughts and you will control your personality and your destiny.

Dwell on clean and healthy thoughts and your emotional life will become healthy. If you still find yourself entertaining toxic thoughts, despite your best efforts, then begin to pray as never before. Pray for the grace to make your good intentions a reality.

The Twelve Step Program has saved millions of people all over the world. In Step One: the addict realizes that he is powerless over some problem or some chemical substance. Step Two: he also realizes that God has the power to help him. Step Three: he turns his life and his will over to the God of his understanding, believing that God will now do for him what he is not able to do for himself.

This formula has worked for millions of people around the world. They have been liberated from their addictions by following this game plan which involves pure prayer and will training.

Pure prayer is nothing more than the will to give yourself to God. You never have to force feelings of any kind. Feelings follow thoughts at their own pace. Patience obtains all.

TRANSFORMATION OF CHRIST

By Fr. John T. Catoir, JCD | July 3, 2017

According to Father Thomas Radcliff, a former Superior General of the Dominican Order, "This is what the phrase *Transformation in Christ* means: We become, by God's grace, what others need us to be, namely, a 'Living Presence.' We are no longer our natural selves."

The word *transformation* is defined as 'a thorough change in one's manner and appearance'. Becoming more Christlike is a matter of acting with kindness, mercy, and justice. As these acts become habitual, they form one's character and destiny.

Being present to the needs of others implies a commitment. You allow the Lord to live in you and act through you. The transformation in Christ brings about a thorough change in your appearance because your actions profoundly affect the way you appear to others. A Christlike person is admirable and kind.

Father Radcliff tells the story of Pope John XXIII who, in 1960, astonished a group of Jewish dignitaries with this greeting, "Good morning. I am Joseph, your brother."

When he entered the room, he no longer thought of himself as the Pope, but by God's grace, he became what his Jewish guests needed him to be at that moment: a true brother.

The needs of others call for a Christlike response. Cathleen Kaveny, a Catholic writer, described the feelings of the average layperson in these words, "Most Catholics do not encounter God as a solitary individual, but in the context of families, parishes, and the larger Church. We see God's identity enmeshed in a rich texture of rituals and relationships." In other words, we not only see Christ in our neighbors, but we become Christ to our neighbors.

When your self-awareness is tuned into the supernatural, you attain a higher level of understanding. This understanding is not based on feelings but on supernatural facts. It is a matter of faith. Through faith we know that Christ abides in us, always helping us to attend to the needs of others.

The secular world does not think this way. It has forgotten its purpose and direction. We, on the other hand, hold fast to the core wisdom found in the Apostle's Creed, "We believe in the Holy Catholic Church, the Communion of Saints, the forgiveness of sin, the resurrection of the body, and life everlasting Amen."

As Christ-bearers, we are at our best when we are messengers of joy. Jesus said, "In this world, you will have many troubles, but be of good cheer, take heart for I have overcome the world…fear is useless, what you need is trust."

I would like to conclude with my favorite quote from Pope John Paul II, "Christ came to bring joy, joy to children, joy to parents, joy to friends and families, joy to the sick and elderly, indeed Christ came to bring joy to all people. Joy is the keynote messenger of Christianity and the recurring motif of the Gospels. Go therefore and become messengers of joy."

Jesus Christ is within you at this very moment. Imagine Him saying, 'Thank you for trusting Me and allowing Me to live in you. Thank you for the many years of struggle and suffering you have endured to bring My love and joy into the world.'

UNDERSTANDING GOD'S MERCY

By Fr. John T. Catoir, JCD | January 5, 2018

Theology is the science that tries to explain the unexplainable. But you don't need an advanced degree in theology to know that God's mercy does not cancel His justice. His mercy and His justice are one. In theological language, this means that God's justice and mercy are not in opposition to one another. Therein lies the mystery.

There's been a lot of buzz going on in Catholic circles about the meaning of God's mercy. My understanding of God's mercy has been deepened by studying the distinction between sins of weakness and sins of malice.

Sins of weakness include addictions of every kind. Addictions are forbidden by God in order to protect us from hurting ourselves. In these matters, God's mercy is like a mother's love. Mothers want you to enjoy your precious life, not destroy it. God is merciful and quick to forgive.

Sins of malice, on the other hand, are malevolent and filled with hatred. Take for instance the Satanic, murderous attack by Muslim Jihadists on the Coptic Christians as they were worshipping. Such sins are straight from hell. Before they can be forgiven, there must be full repentance, including a firm purpose of amendment. God is just. Satan was cast out of heaven for his rebellion.

Pope Francis has stressed the importance of understanding God's mercy because many good Catholics have become scrupulous. Terrified of God, they fear for their salvation. St. Catherine of Siena received these words from God in a private revelation, "Your capacity to sin can never exhaust my capacity for mercy." This message needs to be better known. We should always trust the love and mercy of Our Savior.

When it comes to sins of malice, God is dealing with hostility. "The reason Jesus came was to destroy the works of the devil," (1 John 3:8). His justice will not be mocked. Jesus did not come to destroy the ones doing evil works, quite the opposite. He came, "Not to condemn but to save." (John 3:17) His warnings are meant to be medicinal. A dose of fear can be salvific.

All sin must be repented. Sins of malice especially so, since they are committed with the full consent of the will and they cause great suffering in the process. True repentance requires a firm purpose of amendment and a complete repudiation of one's evil actions and intentions.

The existence of hell has been well established in Sacred Scripture, where it is mentioned many times. Here is one quote from Jesus: "Then He will say to those on His left, 'Depart from Me you cursed, enter the eternal fire prepared for the devil and his followers.'" (Matthew 25:41)

Pope Francis has often stressed God's mercy because many churchmen in the past have abused their authority by constantly preaching fear and damnation. The emphasis is on the word 'constantly'. But Jesus was adamant about encouraging His followers, "not to be afraid." Though the issue is complex, the remedy is in trusting God's wisdom, love, and compassion.

 Listen to these words from Jesus: "Therefore, do not worry about tomorrow, for tomorrow will take care of itself. Each day has enough trouble of its own." (Matthew 6:34)

May the Lord be your strength and your joy.

WHAT DOES JESUS ASK OF YOU
By Fr. John T. Catoir, JCD | June 15, 2018

Jesus asks you to strive for holiness. Don't be anxious. Leave the past to His mercy, the future to His providence, and live in the present moment.

Jesus asks you to strive for holiness. Be Kind. A holy person avoids being unkind, unhelpful, unfriendly, unfeeling, unsympathetic and uncaring.

Jesus asks you to strive for holiness. Cheer up! In this world, you will have many troubles; cheer up anyway. Ask the Lord to give you His strength and joy.

Jesus asks you to strive for holiness. Be on guard against false prophets. By their fruits you will know them. Choose wisely those whom you rely on and trust.

Jesus asks you to strive for holiness. Be willing to make sacrifices. A holy person is ready to give up personal preference to help another. Ask for God's help.

Jesus asks you to strive for holiness. Accept your imperfections of face and body. Attain real beauty by becoming a loving person. Don't spoil your beauty by self-loathing.

Jesus asks you to strive for holiness. Control your tongue. Angry words can hurt deeply. Better to say nothing than to inflict pain. Try to be more sensitive.

Jesus asks you to strive for holiness. Love one another. Be especially kind to family members and respect the elderly.

Jesus asks you to strive for holiness. Respect Mary, His mother. He said, "Behold your Mother to St. John from the cross. She is now our spiritual Mother with authority.

Jesus asks you to strive for holiness. He said, "Learn of Me, for I am One who serves." Serving others is a sign of holiness.

Jesus asks you to strive for holiness. Do not kill. Do not be among those who support the ruthless killing of innocent unborn infants. Be clean of heart.

Jesus asks you to strive for holiness. Curb your anger. Life will be less difficult if you pray with perseverance for the grace to remain calm.

Jesus asks you to strive for holiness. Be nice to your neighbors, even if you don't agree with their politics. Holiness is agreeing to disagree.

Jesus asks you to strive for holiness. Be not unbelieving, but believe. God really loves you. Don't give this truth lip service.

Jesus asks you to strive for holiness. Always believe in the forgiveness of sin, especially your own. Suffer the humiliation of going to confession from time to time.

Jesus asks you to strive for holiness. Love yourself. Temptations are not sins. You are not your thoughts. You are the observer of your thoughts. Reject the bad ones over and over.

Jesus asks you to strive for holiness. Love the divine nature of the Church. Pray for fallen priest and bishops. Even the fallen deserve your kind prayers.

Jesus asks you to strive for holiness. Pray for those who think that the only thing worth living for is their own pleasure and worldly success. Spiritual charity is a sure sign of holiness.

Jesus asks you to strive for holiness. Be courageous. Do not be a coward. Following your bliss can lead to the shirking of duty and responsibility.

Jesus asks you to strive for holiness. Do not be proud. In a family dispute, never forget to choose love over insisting that you're always right.

Jesus asks you to strive for holiness. Be repentant. Always pray for three things: forgiveness of your sins, a continued increase of grace, and the gift of eternal happiness with God in heaven.

WHAT GOD HAS BROUGHT TOGETHER
By Fr. John T. Catoir, JCD | August 14, 2017

Everyone agrees with Jesus, "What God has joined together, let no man put asunder." (Mark 10:9) When a marriage case comes before any Diocesan Tribunal, the question before the Chief Judge is this: Was this marriage joined together by God, or not? In other words, the presumption of validity can be challenged.

If the presumption of validity turns out to be false, the contract can be annulled. An annulment is merely an authorized statement that the marriage contract is not legally valid. The Church grants thousands of annulments worldwide every year because of contractual invalidity.

The grounds for an annulment vary. For example, if one party never intended a permanent union, or an exclusive union, it is "fraud going to the heart of the contract". Having a hidden mistress from day one is a breach of contract.

Before 1960, annulments were rare. The records show that most small dioceses only produced one or two annulments a year. Petitioners were turned away in droves. Judges were hamstrung by canonical laws that reduced the flow of cases to a near standstill.

In response to the widespread feeling of unfairness, the Canon Law Society of America and Canada appointed a special committee to study the whole issue. In 1968, they came up with a plan for reform and presented 27 Norms to the American Bishops.

A year later the U.S. Hierarchy made a few edits and forwarded these norms to the Holy See for approval. To everyone's relief, Rome approved 23 norms of the 27 norms, and gave us permission to begin implementing them in July of 1970. This approval was granted for an experimental period of three years. It was later extended.

Many of the reform items had to do with the specific procedures that caused needless delay. For instance, in understaffed Tribunals, permission was given to appoint one judge to hear each case instead of the normal three-judge panel. This expedited the process considerably.

We also learned about new grounds for granting an annulment. A 1968 case in the *Monitor Ecclesiasticus Vol. II,* reported a breakthrough decision made by a Judge on the Roman Rota. The annulment was based on "immaturity". The judge made a distinction between appreciative knowledge and mere conceptual knowledge of marital consent.

"Immaturity" as grounds for an annulment was unheard of before 1970. In the past, so many petitioners who had a legitimate case were turned away because of canonical rigidity. This should tell you that judging the validity of marital consent is not an exact science.

I mention all this by way of background to the controversy you may have been reading about between two contending forces in the Vatican on the issue of divorce and remarriage. Pope Francis and a clear majority of Cardinals prefer "mercy". A small minority of opponents stress canonical rigidity.

Pope Francis is right. The word "mercy" doesn't change the doctrine of indissolubility. Marriage is a life-long commitment. Neither does it approve of adultery. It merely means that the Spirit of Mercy should infuse our use of the latest jurisprudence.

By offering a second chance to people in need, and looking after the well-being of children, we are offering justice tempered with mercy. Jesus said, "Help bear one another's burdens." (Galatians 6:2)

WHEN A WORKAHOLIC RETIRES

By Fr. John T. Catoir, JCD | March 15, 2018

There is no one more fidgety than a workaholic who is about to retire. Strangely enough, the fear of loneliness is often the unconscious cause of hyperactivity. Being idle, bored, and empty with no activity to occupy your time can be a terrifying experience.

Here's a question for you: is being a workaholic a good thing? After all, if it helps you to make a living, support your family, and give you a sense of purpose – it's a good thing, right? But what if it turns you into a compulsive robot; one who is too busy to live a life of emotional comfort, enjoying your family and friends? Can that be a good thing? I don't think so, especially if it starts to affect your health.

Jesus once said, "I have not come to condemn the workaholic, but to save him" – or words to that effect. It's essentially a spiritual problem.

St. Augustine put it in a few words: "Our hearts are restless until they rest in Thee, O Lord." Something is missing in all of us. A disturbing feeling wells up in us. We feel better if we keep busy doing things that distract us from facing certain fears.

The urge to avoid the fear of loneliness has driven many a good person to drink. Billions of people down through the ages have tried to solve this problem, but have failed to do so. Unfortunately, it's not an easy problem to solve. The natural feeling of isolation is part of every life. Even those who are gifted with the love of a good spouse experience loneliness from time to time.

We all need to understand that even a loving spouse cannot eliminate the problem of loneliness. The need for God is a constant in everyone's life. Try as you may, you cannot make it go away. We keep yearning for more; the reason being that God alone can fulfill the soul's desire for Divine Love. We are searching for something more than mere physical satisfaction. It's a metaphysical problem. Loneliness is the price we pay for being unique. Think about it. Once we leave our mother's womb we are utterly alone in the universe, essentially separate from every other human being.

Some have called it a "nostalgia for paradise," which is in a part true, but it's more a congenital need for an intimacy with God.

The go-go-go rat-race of this world cannot even begin to satisfy these deeper needs. Those who don't understand this problem tend to misdiagnose it and fall into a variety of dangerous behaviors: over-eaters, alcoholics, those engaged in sexual promiscuity, compulsive workaholics, they're all the victims of loneliness gone amok.

Those who do not accept the fact that they crave God's consolation often begin looking for love in all the wrong places. Searching to find relief in sexual promiscuity is like drinking salt water when you're dying of thirst. It does more harm than good.

God is drawing you to Himself through a process of self-discovery. It will go much better for you if you diagnose the process properly. The acceptance of loneliness as a precious gift will sanctify your soul.

Once you are willing to be drawn into intimacy with God, your life will change for the better. Your prayer life will mature, your temperament will become calmer, and your relationship with God will be more loving.

Then your capacity for joy will increase and you will experience a higher zest for life. Rejoice in His love now and enjoy the Lord. Holiness will surely follow.

May the Lord be your strength and your joy.

YOU AND YOUR BIBLE

By Fr. John T. Catoir, JCD | February 12, 2018

An unknown Jewish carpenter came on the scene 2000 years ago and delivered a message that has transformed the lives of billions of people. Hundreds of prophecies in the Hebrew Bible testify to the coming of the Messiah, and Jesus fulfilled them all. The New Testament presents eyewitness accounts of His ministry on earth.

I'm always amazed at how many people find the Bible impossible to believe. That's primarily the fault of modern day scripture scholars who in recent years have introduced so much doubt and division.

The most important guide you can have for the interpretation of the Bible is the Nicene Creed which we recite at Mass. "I believe in God, the Father Almighty, Creator of heaven and earth, and in Jesus Christ, His only Son, born of the Virgin Mary, suffered under Pontius Pilate, was crucified, died and was buried. On the third day, He rose again according to the Scriptures."

In 1988, Cardinal Ratzinger, who later became Pope Benedict XVI, wrote a book entitled *Biblical Interpretation in Crisis*, where he warned against the errors of modern scripture scholars. He said they rely heavily on Immanuel Kant (1724–1804), the famous German skeptic, who developed a method of interpreting scripture which Ratzinger said, "Undermines the very possibility for the Bible to be itself. We can never interpret Sacred Scripture correctly without using the faith of the Church as our guide."

Kant took an approach to the interpretation of Scripture that was devoid of faith. Up until then, the reading of scripture was pretty much a straightforward exercise of believing the text and accepting the guidance of the Church in the interpretation of the difficult passages. According to Kant, the reader of scripture must first reject all knowledge based on faith, including belief in the divinity of Christ. He also looked upon all the Gospel miracles as mere folk tales. Once you dismiss faith and the authority of the Church and allow the disparate opinions of warring Biblical gurus to take over, you're in trouble.

The Evangelical Christian Churches rejected these new scholars and decided to interpret the entire Bible literally. This approach didn't solve the problem. The sacred texts can not all be interpreted literally. The Scriptures are full of metaphors, parables, and figures of speech.

Jesus spoke Aramaic, a language that uses a lot of hyperbole. To make a point, an Aramaic person would probably exaggerate. Jesus told us to forgive "70 times 7". This is the equivalent of saying, 'Let there be no limit to your willingness to forgive.' Sometimes the exact meaning of a text is clear, sometimes it's not. We need the objective authority of the Church to keep us on the right path.

"I believe in the Holy Catholic Church, the communion of saints, the forgiveness of sin, the resurrection of the body, and life everlasting. Amen."

The Church has a human element. To err is human. We also have a Divine element, which protects us from the humans who go astray. Our tradition going back to the formative Christian community, and to Jesus Christ himself, has protected us from doctrinal errors for over 2000 years.

May the Lord be your strength and your joy as you enjoy reading your Bible.

YOUR HIGHER CALLING
By Fr. John T. Catoir, JCD | May 10, 2018

You have a higher calling to present the face of Christ to your loved ones and neighbors. St. Paul said "That is why all of you brothers and sisters in Christ have the same heavenly call. Turn your minds to Jesus and be faithful as He was faithful to the One who appointed Him." (Hebrews 3:1)

Among all the people in the world, Catholics have a special vocation to bring Christ's peace and joy to those who are anxious about the future. This calling is grounded in the wisdom of Jesus Christ. He taught us to believe in the Communion of Saints, the Forgiveness of Sin, the Resurrection of the Body, and in Life Everlasting.

Jesus gave us clarity about our purpose and direction. In ancient times people believed that God spoke to His people through natural catastrophes and we've recently seen the worst of them in the Hawaiian volcanoes and earthquakes. We know better than to allow the storms of life to drive us to despair. Many live in a state of dread. The question hangs over their head, 'what's going to happen next?' With the economy, with North Korea, China and Iran, how will it all end?

You are called to bring the calm assurance of Jesus who said, "In this world you will have many troubles, but be of good cheer for I have overcome the world." (John 16:33)

This is a call to courage. Jesus asks you to be calm. All this confusion will pass. By accepting His challenge, you will find a new personality emerging within you. Your transformation in Christ will have begun in earnest. A joy will come to you that this world cannot give. Even if you feel unworthy and weak, Christ will supply you with his strength and joy.

St. Paul tells you to "Rejoice always!" (Philippians 4:4) Try it and you'll begin to believe that joy is possible. It is both a gift and a choice. You already received the Spirit of Joy at your Baptism when the Lord came to live in you. It's a choice because you need to claim it again and again every day. The Lord will do for you, many things you cannot yet do for yourself. "Fear is useless, what you need is trust." (Luke 8:50)

Trust will enable you to live intimately with the Lord and "Show others that you are a letter from Christ, not written with ink but with the Spirit of God, not on tablets of stone but on the tablets of human hearts." (2 Corinthians 3:3)

If Jesus were here today, He would say, "Thank you for the many years of service and struggle that you have given, and for the suffering you have endured for Me and for the sake of the Kingdom. Thank you for being my voice in a world gone slightly mad. You have allowed the Holy Spirit to act through you, thereby lightening the burdens of others. Be assured, I will help you every step of the way. I will be your strength and your joy."

May God bless you and yours always and forever.

YOUR NEW YEAR'S RESOLUTION

By Fr. John T. Catoir, JCD | November 24, 2017

One of the best ways to be faithful to the Lord is to take him at his word: "Be not afraid." This is a call to courage. Jesus is asking you to be calm in the storm of life, not only for your own peace of mind, but for the well-being of your loved ones. You can decide to present the face of Christ to them by showing them your faith in His strength.

It's normal to worry about the future. The threat of war looms all around us. North Korea, Iran, Isis—they all pose serious threats to our peace. We don't have a crystal ball to tell us what's going to happen next, but we do have a body of wisdom that saves us from a lot of confusion and dread. It's synopsized for us in the Apostles' Creed.

If you're searching for a New Year's resolution, why not avail yourself of the revelations that shape our destiny and purpose in life? All our spiritual knowledge is grounded in the wisdom of Jesus Christ. He said, "In this world you will have many troubles, but take heart and be of good cheer, for I have overcome the world." (John 16:33)

St. Paul wrote, "All of you who are believers have the same divine calling: to turn your minds to Jesus, the High Priest. And be faithful, as He was faithful to the one who appointed Him; namely, His heavenly Father." (Hebrews 3:1)

Here is a plan worth adopting. Jesus urged you to brush aside your fears by focusing on Him and His power to carry you through the storms of life. His teachings, handed down to us from the Apostles, contain a body of knowledge which we need today. By reciting the Apostles' Creed once a day, you will strengthen your faith immensely.

"I believe in God, the Father Almighty, Creator of heaven and earth. I believe in Jesus Christ, His only begotten Son, who was conceived by the Holy Spirit, born of the Virgin Mary, suffered under Pontius Pilate, was crucified, died, and was buried. He descended to the dead, and on the third day He rose again. He ascended into heaven, is seated at the right hand of the Father, and will come again to judge the living and the dead. I believe in the Holy Spirit, the Holy Catholic Church, the communion of saints, the forgiveness of sins, the resurrection of the body, and life everlasting. Amen."

Your decision, to recite this Creed once a day will help you to trust the Lord in all circumstance. Your gradual transformation in Christ will bring blessings to those whom you love, and earn you a higher place in heaven. Why not trust the Lord? He will do for you what you are not yet able to do for yourself: Be not afraid.

May the Lord be your strength and your joy.

YOUR TAX DOLLARS

By Fr. John T. Catoir, JCD | October 14, 2017

The First Amendment's Right to Religious Freedom is sacred and must be upheld. In the same First Amendment, the right to express a grievance against any violation of religious freedom is also guaranteed.

We believe in the dignity of every human life. Why have we been forced to pay our hard-earned tax dollars to the government when they use it to finance millions of abortions?

Down through the years, Planned Parenthood has received about $500 million a year in taxpayer dollars. To be exact, they received $528 million last year according to their own annual report. In 2013, their CEO admitted to receiving an annual compensation of $590,928, and that figure has been going up each year.

In one year, the period between 2013–2014, Planned Parenthood's annual report indicated that they killed 327,653 preborn infants. We find even one abortion to be morally abhorrent. How long can this go on?

In a recent column I wrote about the success of the joint challenge of the Little Sisters of the Poor, the Texas Baptist University and five other litigants, who challenged the Constitutionality of the Obamacare contraceptive mandate. It is officially called the Patient Protection and Affordable Care Act. It was passed by the 111th U.S. Congress and signed by President Barack Obama on March 23, 2010.

However, Obamacare soon became unaffordable and failed to protect most of the people it was designed to help. An opposition movement soon became a hot political issue. The Conservative Tea Party held its first "March on Washington" in 2009. The policy of forcing citizens to finance abortions with their taxes dollars was a big concern.

The movement was made up largely of women who tried to bring attention to the disconnect between Congress and the voice of the people. The 2016 election was a referendum on this disconnect.

Our peaceful electoral process was mild compared to the Boston Tea Party of 1773 when a band of colonists, under the leadership of

Samuel Adams and his raiders, came out at midnight disguised as Mohawk warriors and boarded three British cargo ships. They proceeded to dump 343 cartons of tea into the Harbor, shouting, "No taxation without representation!"

This all came about because the colonists had already endured thirteen years of Britain's continued increasing of taxation. The last straw came when the Tea Act of 1773 was imposed. The protest exploded and the stage was set for the American Revolution. The rest is history.

Today a milder storm is brewing over the government's funding of abortion services. It's NOT about a woman's right to have an abortion in a clean medical facility. It's about forcing taxpayers to finance actions they deem to be immoral. This amounts to an unconstitutional First Amendment violation.

We have always believed in supporting the common good through a fair system of taxation. This is our patriotic duty. But after seeing our religious rights being disregarded for decades, we find it necessary to issue a firm protest.

May the Lord be your strength and your joy as you deal with this problem in your respective Congressional districts.

YOU CAN FIND MORE FROM FR. JOHN CATOIR AT:

Website: www.johncatoir.com
YouTube: Fr. John Catoir – Messenger of Joy!
Facebook: Fr. John Catoir
Twitter: Fr. John Catoir, JCD